T0208477

How to find love

The only relationship book you need

Helena Källström

BALBOA.
PRESS
A DIVISION OF HAY HOUSE

Balboa Press books may be ordered through booksellers or by contacting:

Balboa Press
A Division of Hay House
1663 Liberty Drive
Bloomington, IN 47403
www.balboapress.com
1 (877) 407-4847

Print information available on the last page.

ISBN: 978-1-9822-0981-0 (sc)
ISBN: 978-1-9822-0980-3 (hc)
ISBN: 978-1-9822-0982-7 (e)

Library of Congress Control Number: 2018909200

Balboa Press rev. date: 08/21/2018

I dedicate this book to

Nicole the light of my life that makes everything possible. She is the one who tells me to just do it. You are true love and light and so smart and you can do everything you want. I am the proudest mom.

Sara thank you for all the laughs. Your ambitions are going to take you around the world and back and you will accomplish greatness.

Kim a gift from the past. Kim you are such a rare person, so unique and so special. And you absolutely have the best sense of humour.

Frida pretty please the wild one. There is no doubt in my mind that your charm is going to take the world with storm.

Dear reader,

Welcome to a journey on how to find love. This book is about the amazing power you have to create and build the life that you seek. How to change your perspective from fear to love that will give you a positive influence on your relationships and your own well being. The book is for all of you seeking the right partner or has a tendency to find the "wrong one", it is for you who don't know if you should stay or if you should go. But it is also for you who feels an emptiness or longing for something more in your life.

The book is easy to read and full of questions and tips that can help you find the answers to more love in your life.

Contents

Foreword

I feel Disney magic every time the first snowflakes fall. Great beauty and not a snowflake like another. Equally astonished am I to see the first spring flowers pop up, Snowdrops, Scilla, Crocus and Anemones. It's the typical Swedish sign that winter is finally leaving. Then come summer and the amazing feeling of grass beneath my bare feet's. In august I love to swim in the warm velvety ocean at dusk. I like to watch the intense shades of leaves that fall in October that evokes childhood memories of wanting to jump in piles of leaves. The same strong loving feelings are awakening by the scent of freshly harvested tomatoes, strawberries and apples. Or when I listen to music that lifts my soul and makes me dance in the kitchen or an intense color that attracts my attention. It all creates a heaven for my senses and my feelings.

Perhaps I feel like this because we humans are made of energy in the form of vibrations and frequencies that are raised and lowered and these in particular creates magic in the form of love in my body and soul? Perhaps this is what I have chosen to believe in? Or this is what I have created to be my truth and my definition of happiness and love.

We can always choose to create our lives with more magic and love. We have the ability to influence and change a lot more than we usually think that we can. And it is all about what we believe is true, we create our world with our thoughts. Our beliefs and our values becomes our reality and are what we manifest. What happens outside of us happens within us. When I was young, I loved to watch the stars. A feeling of guidance and that someone or something could see my greatness. Have you ever felt the magic feeling when you look up at the starry August sky or on a sparkling clear winter night? I feel a belonging to the infinity mass of stars? A feeling that is totally free from fear.

When it comes to relationships we usually don't think about what it is we are really manifesting with our thoughts, we spend time to dream or hope that miracles like love should come from someone else.

What will happen if much of what we have learned to "believe" in is not true? What happens to ourselves when we begin to question our truths, our values and our beliefs? What happens when we look farther than our fears? And what will happen if we change our thoughts? It may even be that we will find the greatest love of them all.

Introduction

I have for a long time believed that when only the greatest love of them all, "the one", shows up, everything will workout just fine. Then I will have the prefect relationship and live happily ever after. And perhaps when the right partner shows up all the pieces in the puzzle will fall into the right place. Maybe I will feel that I have found my other half, my soul selected. But to tell you the true's I have already thought that a number of times and then I have become disappointed when it turned out that were not the case.

I also believed that my relationships were based on a feeling of deep love. I thought that we knew each other, that we were quit honest and authentic. Then I realized I was wrong. It wasn't true love, it was terms and conditions, it was a lot of expectations and it all origin from fear. It was mine and others beliefs of how it should be and how it should feel.

With time, I have learned that relationships require a lot of work, it requires us to meet one another fearlessly, with great trust and with great love and that we ourselves create opportunities for personal development and growth. And I have also learned that in life we often grow at different pace and it might not be that we should stay with one partner for the rest of our life.

We all need relationships even if the meaning of them can be different for us. And I am absolute certain that we can become whole as we so often long for using the missing piece. But it is not the missing piece that makes us whole. It is I myself that makes me whole, using the missing piece in positive terms. There is nothing outside of me that can change what is inside of me. The love that I seek is within me. If I think someone else will make me whole, fill the void and give me all the love I need I am fooling myself. We are all entitled to perfect love. But we are looking for love in imperfect relationships with imperfect people. It leaves us frustrated, disappointed and with a sense of emptiness and a search for someone else. A search that rarely gives us what we need.

Love is the greatest source that can put us in connection with everything and everyone. Love is what gives us the air under our wings. An intense and deep feeling towards anyone or anything but the quality of the love we get depends on how we really feel. Love is something we often dream about it's our hearts deepest desire. We seek, we yearn, we want love but we miss very often that we need to start with our innermost. To feel loved, we need to love ourselves.

In a time of hugely popular films like the Twilight trilogy with a feeling of being selected by a person who loves us forever, we get a blooming dream of the absolute romantic relationship. Do you know that "to be chosen" is the most common dream by most women? We want to be selected as the one and only. Paradoxically, it turns out that it is usually the woman who chooses the man. After the premiere of the much-publicized film 50 Shades of Grey circulated a text on Facebook. It read, this movie is romantic just because the man is rich, if it had been a poor man who lived in a trailer; it had been an episode of Criminal Minds. And if I personally review 50 Shades of Grey, I don't feel that the film is romantic, it is rather tragic and yet there is a desire to be submissive to a man in control. Again, we are back to wanting to be the chosen woman who gets all the love out of one single man.

Most of us want monogamous loving relationships. From a female perspective, there is usually nothing more unattractive than a man dating a lot of different women. As a man it is more common to have another view in the matter (generalizing). These common patterns comes from our origin of the man as the hunter and woman as the one who takes care of the children and are depending on a man who comes home with food and supplies. Our past remains in our DNA and make it selves occasionally reminded without us even thinking about it. Moreover, we have when we go into a relationship with us patterns from our upbringing, values, and the norms of society and so on. And to this we can add our differences as men and women both psychologically and physiologically.

Love is a powerful force, it is wonderful, but what happens when we do not find what we are looking for and what is it we are searching for? Or when the ongoing love no longer feels like we think it should feel? Why do most people in our society chase love even though it is possible to live a good life alone? And why are those who are divorced/separated so eager to commit again? What are we looking for? Why are we not happy? Why do we constantly seek a new love and why do we feel incomplete? What can fill the void that we carry in our heart?

Most of us are basically looking for security, success, wealth, status, power, recognition, praise and love, all of which are a way to fill the gaping hole within us, a hole formed by our separation from the love of ourselves. If love is so central to whom we are and what we need why are we often so far away from it? Why do we put cotton and high protection around our heart instead of showing our vulnerability? Neither do we believe that we can be loved for who we are, but we prevent ourselves from trusting love. This is a major dilemma for us. One side of us hunger for love, while we at the same time refuse to open ourselves totally to receive love.

We can keep on searching for someone else that will fill the yearning hole that is within us. Someone who loves me above all else and give me the pink shimmering life that I want. But this expectation often leads to disappointment. The most important relationship we have is the one to ourselves, that's the simple truth. As long as we do not realize it, we will be unhappy or continue to search for the perfect partner. When I meet a partner I meet my own positive and negative sides. We meet our reflection. When the less favourable sides come to the surface, we have the ability to blame our partner, we are blaming the one we have chosen to love us.

We limit ourselves with our own thoughts and it prevents us from developing and move forward as it often stems from fear. Fear of the unknown, fear from the past, fear of the future and of changes. And if we are afraid we are fighting against the fear. We start feeling a resistance. We may even begin to believe that it is something wrong with our partner if he/she do not think and look at things in the same way as we do. Our personal ego wants to be right, and we may have a feeling of loosing control and a fear of what we don't know or don't want to know and all that fear creates its Fort Knox around us. We begin to build walls of protection and not letting our partner near and it is creating a bigger gap between us. If we instead can get to the bottom of the fear itself and see its origin, we can change the feeling that changes the thought to come from love instead.

In this book we will explore what it is that makes us feel incomplete, why we are searching for love and validation outside of ourselves. What is affecting us and what we can do to change our own behaviour to achieve the love we yearn for? To do this, we will start in a very different end, namely in the world of quantum physics.

The World of Quantum Physics

Existence is pulsating energy. Everything from the body, soul, objects and even money is energy. Energy vibrates; it has a frequency or a resonant. These different wave lengths are the key to being able to achieve everything you want. And if the intellect is made of energy, it means that even your thoughts and emotions are energy which consists of frequencies. And like when you are listening to the radio you can change to a better channel.

You vibrate at frequencies that are harmonious and uplifting and frequencies that are dissonant and have a negative impact. It is quite easy to understand that one thought has one frequency, another thought has another frequency, and that your thought and feelings affects your own and other people's energy fields. If you send out negative thoughts that have low frequency energy you can never attract a higher energy if you do not change your own frequency. It's you who has to put your self in a more positive state of mind to receive positive energy from anyone else. Equally frequencies attract each other while different frequencies repel each other. In meeting with other people you can easily notice someone else's energy field, you can feel alive or you can feel drained.

The journalist Lynne McTaggart, has written a book called, The Field; The Quest for the Secret Force of the Universe. It is written by scientific experiment to the conclusion that life holds a bearing, underlying energy field that is responsible for our minds highest functions. They call this field the Zero Point Field. Zero Point Field is a higher collective consciousness that makes it possible for us to have the whole universe within us and with practice retrieve all the information that is stored in the field. And that it is the human intentions that make the field so powerful. It is your thoughts, feelings and actions. Zero Point Field connects everything. It looks like a void around you but in this, to the eye, empty spaces are infinite possibilities. The only difference between you and all that you want to achieve is energy frequency. The only difference between you and other living organisms and material are void (zero field).

According to Albert Einstein's quantum physical theories, there is no existence of what you today perceive as vertical time. Einstein's theories explain that there is no difference between past, present and future, this is only an illusion. And what does all of this have to do with relationships and love? Shortly you will see the connection between quantum physics and how you can change your self to get better relations.

If time as we perceive it is an illusion, it means that everything co-exists here and now. The frequency that you send out with your thoughts and feelings go where your attention is directed. When you want to achieve new results, you are already the result. You receive what you send out. This allows you to get what you want.

If you are thinking about if you are worthy or not worthy something, you put a grade on what you deserve and do not deserve. What you are telling your self is that you are worthy some tings and not others. If you have a slightest hidden thought that you are not worthy what you want or desire it will not come true. Take a pair of shoes as an example, if you start think about if you are worthy a new pair of shoes, there is usually a little voice in you head that says, stop there, have you earned this, or do you really need them? In a microscopic second you have doubts and it makes you hesitate. If you instead think these shoes are gorgeous they are mine. Then your wish comes from a deeper inner conviction without any hidden doubt. Can you see the difference? It's a much deeper level without any hesitation and it doesn't give you any regrets. But in life you may have learned that material things are important and you buy a lot of things that you don't need so doubts and regrets are part of every day life. And when you choose relationship you may choose dysfunctional relationships because your choices don't come from your deepest, loving conviction, it comes from fear and an unclear energy. And how many times do you value your self and your life through the reflection of others?

The Law of Attraction

As an adult, it can be difficult to believe in a magical bond to an invisible world that works for your own account. But believe me, you can do magic with your thoughts. The law of attraction is all about your own power to manifest what you desire.

To understand the law of attraction, you need to assume that you live on three different levels.

You live in the physical (your body) you live in the psychological (thoughts and feelings) and you live in the spiritual (which I call a higher consciousness). However, different belief systems see spirituality in different ways, so it depends on what you believe in. Some believe that meditation is equal to spirituality some think it is mumbo-jumbo or that you must believe in reincarnation to be spiritual. There are many different variations of answers to what spirituality is. For me, spirituality is to be connected to something larger, outside myself. To be connected with what is, in the zero-point field. For me, it would also explain to some level the search for the missing pieces of the puzzle in the form of love outside of us. That we actually are connected with something "slightly" larger but we don't have the knowledge of how to use this field.

The law of attraction says that what you send out, you get back, whether it is positive or negative. You use this law every second, every day. For it to work as you want, you need to "place an order", believe in it and receive. To do this, you need not only be sure of what it is you want, but you need to be absolutely convinced that this is what you want. Your request is sent to the universe and the universe responds to your thoughts and feelings. Your thoughts/feelings consist of energy that makes the universe perceive them. But again, you must know exactly what you want and be completely convinced of this. If you are not completely sure the universe will get an ambiguous frequency and then sends back an undesirable result. As soon as you think or say; I hope, but…, or…. there will be a rapid automatic thought which tells you that you are not worthy and you do not get your order filled. We all have rapid/fast automatic thoughts, old programming that makes us hesitant about whether we really deserve what we ask for. It is your underlying wounds and memories that you often have created a long time ago.

For example, you are driving in your car, looking for a parking space and are thinking positive thoughts. "I will find a parking space near the entrance." Chances are much greater that you will find a parking space close to the entrance than if you think negatively. "I want a parking space near the entrance but I will not get one because it is always occupied".

In your search for relationships, you are often quick to send out negative thoughts and feelings. I want him/her but he/she is not interested in me, I'm not good enough, he/she does not want someone like me, etc. Do you recognize you're self in these thoughts? If you think that something will work out, it will usually be all right, if you think that something will go wrong, it will usually go wrong - the law of attraction.

Once you're convinced of what you want. Place your order to the universe. Your order should be made by both your thought and pronounced aloud or written down. Send a mental image or express clearly what it is you want. Think of what you want as it is already yours, whether it's about a new job, to get well or a new/better relationship. The more detailed vision you have the better. Then imagine your self in the situation. How does it feel in the new workplace, how do you feel in your healthy body. How do the man/woman you are searching for feel next to you etc? It is very important not to use negations. A negation is for an example; I will not gain weight, think in terms of, I am or I feel healthy or I am or feel slim. Close your eyes and imagine that your order has already come true. You must act, speak and think as if you have already received what you ordered. Then have trust that the universe will arrange what is best for you.

If you need to keep an eye on, or wonder if this will happen, you are telling the universe that you do not have faith that it will happen and you will not attract what you desire. Have patience. Do not stress over how it will be done, let the universe do it for you. When you are trying to control, you lack faith in the universe (the universe, god, the higher self or whatever is suitable for you).

You can not order an absolutely fantastic relationship if there is chaos within yourself. You can never order prosperity in life if you constantly radiate a frequency of poverty. Poverty is not always lack of money, poverty may well have to do with how you feel and think in connection with money or wealth. You can not get more than what you yourself are prepared to receive. And how much you are prepared to receive depends on how much you have worked through your wounds. Are you with me? You choose which world you are going to attract and attend.

You send an order from you and when the order leaves you it sends a wave of opportunities in the future, you can call the wave your determination of energy. When the wave then reaches the future, the future sends an echo wave back in time to confirm that it is received. The two waves moving forward and back in time can integrate in several different ways in the present. They can neutralize each other and they can reinforce each other. In other words, you have waves of possibilities (thoughts, feelings, actions) that go back and forth. The waves can be crossed and integrated with each other anywhere in what is called an interference pattern that stabilizes the frequency depending on what you are thinking.

Everything that appears to be solid material is in fact stable frequency. Your outer world is a projection of your inner world. Do you understand why it is so important to formulate your order (determination) in the present tense, to create your order as if it already exists? It is important to let your attention stay at the goal no matter what happens. Don't start to doubt it.

Summary;

Decide what it is you want to order? As soon as you have placed an order it already exists on the spiritual plane (you have sent out the order in the form of thoughts and feelings). You need to feel and express the order in words, either on paper or verbally so it realizes at the psychological level. Physically - you have to act in accordance as you have already received what you ordered.

Modern physicists believe that everything in the universe is basically pulsating energy that happens to be transformed as certain configurations of matter at certain times. Especially in the observation moment, that is, at the moment when your consciousness happens to concretize it. Are you with me why quantum physics plays a big role in your life? You create everything that happens around you through your thoughts, feelings and actions. If you have the intention to create a change in your relationships you need to know what potential you have to change. And that the potential lies in your own thoughts. It is only you that can change your life.

I do not think you are trying to find something that you never had. I think you are trying to bring back something that you miss. We are often taught in the modern society that we are not complete in ourselves. It is the norm that we believe in. But the norm is created and we can change it. Some of you are probably hesitating now thinking, I do not get everything that I want and manifests. Then let me take it a step further, and I am aware that there are those of you who don not believe in the same things as I do, if you are one of them, then you can skip my theories and move on to the next chapter.

I think there is a higher level, that you are destined to meet the people that you meet for you to learn. Not just in the meeting with the individual who can give you pretences to heal. This "something" can be different things that you need to take you further in your own development. Lessons you need to learn. And for you to be able to do this, it must be pre-determined before you are born. I have met many people and had many experiences in my life where I immediately felt that there is something more than what the eye can see. It is not a coincidence, there is a greater meaning behind it and I can not dismiss the idea that there is a bigger plan for each one of us. That our souls have an "agreement" to meet and learn that is not created in this life time. I hope that one day we can look back and see a pattern and understand what was the lesson to learn. It's not always easy to see.

In the terms of the law of attraction and that you do not get what you wish could be explained that there is an "agreement", a larger curriculum (also called prarabdha karma) that you are not aware of, which means that you do not get what you wish. Your soul has an agreement that replace your ability to manifest what you want. There is a more important purpose that you do not know about. Maybe you are not the person you are supposed to be yet? Maybe you are not ready?

Personally, I often forget to ask for what I need. But that's not all, often so I do not even notice what I have created. But guess what? I think you are like me, manifesting much more than you think. Try to write down everything good and bad that has happened to you in a week and explores how many of the events that you could predict would happen or which of them you have asked for? Remember when you were little and wrote your wishes to Santa Claus? My niece writes wish lists from toy catalogs and often there is a doll on the list. "Oh, just the doll I wished" for, she exclaims, and shines like the sun when she opened a gift wrap of the content that she wants. Do you remember that feeling? Your ability to manifest is always present.

Relationships A Journey of Discovery and Self-Knowledge

If we look back historically, we have erased many of the differences between the feminine and the masculine energy (more on this subject later). My grandparents lived with an old traditional distribution of gender roles, even though there was also common for women to some extent to join the workforce at least until they had children. From that perspective, we were only half people who were dependent on the other half to be able to reproduce and get food on the table. Men have needed women, women have needed men in order to survive. Today, we are not dependent in the same way by a partner (except for sexual reproduction).

But when it comes to intimate relationships, we often believe that we are still half without a partner. There is a great risk with thinking like this. If we do not feel like a whole person, the lack of something that someone else will bring us makes us dependent on another human being to survive. If I become dependent on you, then I will constantly be afraid of loosing you. When fear controls, we honestly do not make the best choices for ourselves. If someone else will provide me with love, it's pretty easy to start seeing that person as an object and not as a love. And an object needs to be controlled by control, force or manipulation. Chances are we become frustrated and disappointed and then we try changing the other person to better meet our needs, and if that does not work maybe we settle for less than what we are worth. And if that does not work either, we try to find someone else who will live up to our expectations. Having relationships based on dependence leads to resentment, anger, frustration and disappointment because there is no person who can fulfil all that we desire.

How many times have you believed that you have found the right one? Finally someone who understands you and in the beginning of the relationship you dare to be quite open, but then fear is slowly creeping in. What will happen, if you say what you really think or feel, maybe he/she might leave you? So instead you start to reduce or to withhold, you don't expose or tell everything. You do it because it may be associated with losing the one you think you love. At the same time, you may think it's so awesome to finally have found someone that you believe meets all of your needs. Moreover, maybe you try to meet your partner's wishes, but when you try to give someone else what they want, it's often not the things you want or need. After a while, it is common to feel unsure about whether this relationship is right or wrong. And it is possible in a few more years, that the question you ask your self is, who am I?

Some people choose to be alone, and it may be for fear of being betrayed or that they lack the motivation to put time and energy into a relationship but it can also be a way to get back to her/his own strength or that the person actually feel content to be by himself. Sometimes we use different kind of reasons not to enter into a new relationship. My work takes all my energy, I need to focus on the kids right now, and I need space etc. And some of us have used the same phrase to excuse us when we are not interested instead of being honest.

Is it possible to have a relationship that lasts forever and is it really what you want? I am absolutely convinced that it is possible to create relationships that will last forever if both have this common intention. It requires, however, that both parties are prepared to develop together and give each other space. Both have to work with their own fears and dare to prove vulnerable. Often we take the much easier way and give up or move on. The people we meet are our mirror images. It is fantastic that we have been privileged to meet people who can help us learn more than we ever could have imagined. I always say that there is nothing in life that's a coincidence. It is my absolute conviction. The difficulty usually lies in, what am I supposed to learn? When I meet some people the lessons can be very clear to see, in others much more difficult and it often depends on how much fear there are in me. How deep my own wounds are. And many times we do not even see the scars. And this is often why we get problem in our relationships. We become angry and disappointed and we blame it on our partner but oh so wrong we are, if we dare to look deeper. Healing our own wounds and changing our thought patterns is not an easy work to do, because we usually do not even think about what we think, where it comes from and how it affects us. The process can be quite painful, but it's also very liberating. It gives you honesty and freedom and once you feel that feeling you do not want to be without it, it makes you feel like a new, stronger, better version of yourself.

If we go back to the love stage or why you meet those you meet. You do not find your partner by mistake, you have no luck/bad luck, and it's not a coincidence that you meet someone. You fall in love with all her/his positive sides which is actually a reflection of your own positive sides. What you see in her/his character is traits that you like about yourself. If you fall for the security that she/he surround himself with, it is because you feel safe. If you like her/him because she/he is very social, it is a quality that you value in yourself. If you fall for her/his eyes, it is because you recognize something in yourself that you can see in those eyes.

If you find your partners insecurity charming, it is because you recognize yourself in her/his uncertainty. If you fall for the rebel in her/him, there is a rebel in you that wants out (if it is not already out there).

What happens in destructive relationships you ask? I do not have his/her destructive side?

Are you sure? If you are really honest, do you not also have a lot of pretty destructive perhaps even less favourable sides of your self? Or do you only have good qualities? Could it be that the reflection you get out of your partner hides a different feeling? That anger hides uncertainty? That irritation conceals inferiority that rejection hides vulnerability. It all comes down to, love or fear. You face what you love and what you are afraid of in yourself. And many times you meet what feels familiar, what you know and are accustomed to from your past.

You will not meet a more mature partner until you have become more mature. You will not meet a more loving partner until you become a more loving person. You will not meet a more secure partner until you have become safer. Most people who have had repeated relationships confirm that though they have been in love and happy in the beginning it didn't work out better this time than the last. It might not have been the same reason for not continuing to be in the relationship, but it's the same basic issues in them selves that are not processed. You can not escape your own work if you want a change. Each shortcut you try to take, will fail sooner or later. You meet yourself in the reflection of others and it causes different behaviours in you.

What you can do is to work with a partner to heal the wounds which you bear within you to evolve and move forward. Every time you get angry, irritable, sad, criticize, judge, etc. turn inward and find out what is it that makes this "tick "in you? Why are you so hurt? Why are you offended? Why are you so scared? Something has happened to you in the past that makes you react in this way. The answer is always within your self. What if, you instead think that a relationship is the best

13

learning place for you to develop? You can become a whole person in the mirror of someone else. Then you are on the right path. If you also keep in mind that your subconscious governs a reason to your choice of partner. You are very often attracted to someone who you know will meet your emotional needs. You find that someone who is reflecting the self-image that you carry at the moment. Sometimes you meet a man or woman who scares you and impact your whole emotional register. Feelings that is so strong that you do not dare to explore them. It is not uncommon to be terrified of love or even to the thought of going into a relationship. If you instead of remaining in fear, uncertainty, or whatever kind of feeling that pops up within you actually observe them, feel them, and ask for help makes a big difference.

Example on what you can do, right now, when you do/say like this I feel terribly scared, can you help me to find out what is going on within me? If you dare to ask questions like these and ask for help will heal your wounds and slowly the unwanted feelings disappear. It's really courageous and very stimulating and it gives you a better relationship with your self and to others.

If you are like me there are probably many times you just want to run when you become afraid, hurt, offended. But if you stop for a second and consider what it is that others say/do that makes you feel like this. What are the person's intentions? Are they good? Why then, are you afraid? Is the other party really intentionally trying to hurt you? Perhaps that person is, but then the question becomes, what is it that makes you tick? And if you really are getting hurt on purpose should you stay in the relationship? And even if the person is saying/doing things that hurt you, chances are pretty small that it actually is about you, really. It is the other person's own wounds, which makes him or her to hurt you, deliberately or unconsciously. But you should never accept violations or someone doing you harm. It does not matter whether it is conscious or unconscious. I read somewhere that we should never trust anyone who betrays us more than twice. The first time is a warning, the other time it is a lesson and more times then that is simply someone who somehow try to take advantage of us.

Ask yourself, why do I feel this way, is about me? We have the ability to believe that the whole world revolves around ourselves. Haven't we all met a grumpy cashier or someone who is in a very bad mood? Why would that person be mad at you? It's about something else entirely. Why do you believe that it is about you? Or when your partner comes home after a hard days work and take it all out on everyone who comes near. Is it about you? If not, say stop! We need to learn to vent our feelings where they belong. We may need to say that today everything has gone terrible wrong and I feel very irritable and then let it go, or ask if it is okay to spread a lot of negative energy to get it out of your system. Some people are using this way to vent their emotions as a strategy to make the environment annoyed so he/she in good conscience can continue without being challenged? If I get you to be angry, you can not question that I'm pissed. I'm not saying that we shouldn't tell our partner negative things. What I am saying is, what is the reason for spreading negative vibes? Its spreads like ripples in water, is it worth it? The things we can not change, we need to accept and then let go.

Sometimes you meet a partner and entering into a new relationship and there is a lot of signs for wakening up and learning to grasp the lesson. And maybe, this time, too, you ignore it, do not pretend the void or the pain, repress it and you don't take the ownership. You are simply not responsible for your own discomfort. Could it be that you fall in love with the wrong people for the wrong reason? Or maybe you are in a relationship with the right person but you don't know how to love?

Trust issues tend to be common in many relationships. Many of us have lost our confidence on this road, called life. Someone you have trusted has hurt you, and then it is difficult to build up trust again. When you have been exposed to very strong emotional stress and difficult situations you often take a conscious or subconscious decision that says, you should never expose your self to this pain again. Your entire body and soul will do everything that you can not to fall into the same situation again. You do not want the feelings of being hurt so you turn off and you do not leave your self out fully. You won't let anyone near, because you do not have confidence that they actually wish you well. If she/he knows everything about me, maybe she/he thinks I'm weak and that's a risk that seems too great, and she/he will surely leave me. You do not have confidence that someone will like you as you are. And the reason you do not have confidence that someone will like you as you are, is that you do not have the confidence that you are worthy of love. If you instead dared to challenge your problem with trust issues, it could help you to sift the wheat from the bait. If you tell what you feel and the person standing in front of you stays, then it feels like a confident, fearless partner who stands before you. If the person instead is unable to meet you where you are, it may not be the right person for you? What is also good to know is that an unconsciously or consciously emotional decision that you have created under strong emotional stress you can not logically change. It is not enough to know that you have for example trust problems to heal this feeling. You need to feel the origin of this feeling again to be able to change the decision you took at that particular moment. Many of the difficulties you have in a relationship is only the symptom, you need to address the underlying problem. I use energy therapy, helping me to bypass the intellect and find the feeling underneath to heal the wounds.

Energy Therapy is a form of therapy that is performed under light hypnosis or a deep meditative state. You are fully aware and present, and you can bypass the intellect and find the emotions/root of the problems that you have today. It can be a problem with a fragile self-esteem, fear of being left, anxiety, why you can not gain or loose weight, I'm not worthy of love, etc. Everything you react on today is rooted in past experience. I often say that we should stop treating symptoms and find the root of the problem. Once we have found the bottom of the problem, we can heal the emotional wounds that make it difficult for us today. Energy therapy will find our created truths and decisions and then we can change them to be more advantageous and fit the life we live today. You no longer have to be stuck in the consequences of previous negative experiences.

Our life experience enables you to take the wrong decisions today because it origin from old emotional programming, which in turn is reflected in the love of ourselves. A lot of children today grow up with parents who are separated, which often creates a feeling of being left. Once you have been left you do not want to be left again. So you acquire different strategies to not end up in the same place again. You may simply do not go into a new relationship. Or maybe you go into a relationship, but do not stay - better leave first than to be left. You find conscious or unconscious ways not to be disappointed again.

Maybe you stay in a relationship at any price. Friends and family around you are telling you that you don't have a healthy relationship, but you don't listen. It may be due to a deep desire to be loved, to be needed, not wanting to be alone, not believing to be able to provide for you. It could also be because you have found a partner who you know will not disappoint you, and then perhaps it does not really matter how the relationship in general feels like? And it may be that with this particular person, you live a life that you can not sustain yourself- that social status is more important than the relationship.

Why do you stay in relationships that you probably should not stay in? It often has to do with an unconscious programming, that you do not think you are worth more than this. This is probably the best I can get. And sometimes it's because you got used to it, if you experienced it before this is probably how it should be. You need to work a lot with your self-esteem and find the answer to what it is that makes you content with yourself like this? Why is your value not set for the very best for and of you?

It is easy to be blinded in the beginning of a new relationship. Star struck by the other person's lovely, wonderful, positive sides. After a while comes what you perceive as negative sides sneaking in and you begin to hesitate. Is this really right for me? I usually say that one should trust your intuition and that the intuition can not be wrong. But your intuition can be very difficult to read. Some people have a very strong pronounced gut feeling and know at once what is good or bad for them, others have not a clue. A positive feeling that something is right, gives you energy, you feel revitalized. Imagine that you are doing something you love to do. It could be your favourite hobby or anything else that you think is very funny. How does this feel within you? Do you get a warm, lovely, joyful feeling? If you instead do something that will make you repress a part of your self. It could be something that you really don't want to do, something that that you are doing because your partner would like you to participate, but you really don't want to go or something that feels unsafe for you. Something that makes you think, oh what a distress, do I have to? How does this feel within you? As you will be smothered or want to escape? Others have physical sensations of what is good or bad for them. There is a great difference between a positive feeling of happiness fluttering in your stomach or a sense of anxiety. If you do not have a clue on how your gut feeling really fells you need to practice and test until you find it.

I had a conversation with a woman about how difficult it is to know if it is the right relationship or not. I got a long list from her how it felt at the time. Locked, tied, choked, feeling bad, want to escape. Her headache was that she didn't know if she was afraid and it was her own trust issues that were haunting her or if it was her intuition saying this is not right for her. How will you know if it's your intuition or your egos fear? And in the next second she said that this relationship is really worth investing in. Does this feel familiar?? Thoughts that are going back and forth, is this right, is this wrong, should I stay, should I go, how should I know? How do you know? It would be fantastic if there was a 100 percent emotional guaranty when you enter into a relationship, unfortunately, life does not work that way. You usually try and think your way out of the situation. And the more you think, the harder it is to know how it really feels. You end up in a locked position, because you think too much. Take a step back, breathe, release all expectations and try to relax.

Is it possible for you to see relationships as a wonderful journey of discovery? Do you need to go all in with the expectation that it's forever? As long as you do not go against and break your own values. And I emphasis on your own values not someone else's. If you take away all expectations of how it should be, what others think and just go by how it feels, right now. And remain in what feels good for you. If you feel bad and start to lie to conceal the true state of your relationship, you need to take a closer look if this is a relationship that you should stay in or why are you staying?

> Ask yourself questions like;
> Does this make me feel good?
> Is this were I want to be?
> It this the best relationship I could have?
> Am I pleased with the second best?

The Power of Your Thoughts

According to CG Jung's theories of your ego, the ego contains of two parts, a conscious and an unconscious part, the unconscious is called the shadow. The shadow is the sides of yourself that you have, but you do not want to admit, feelings and traits that does not agree with your ego ideal. They are the parts you deny but that still govern your lives. Your shadow makes itself known and reminded every day. The shadow reacts with anger, frustration and other less favourable sides you do not really want. It is only when you become friend and accepts your shadows that you can find your full potential. It is often said that your shadows can be wonderful servant but dangerous master.

According to studies, a human approximately have 40,000 thoughts per day. In 95% of all the decisions that you take, you do it without thinking. It leaves you fully aware of only 5% of your decisions. Your automatic thoughts are not impartial but an attempt of your brain to describe reality based on your previous experiences. By learning to understand your thought patterns you can learn to change them and take new decision and find your authentic, genuine self.

Having control of your life is to become the master of your own thoughts. Listen to your thoughts and move your consciousness to what is empowering you. When you listen to your mental space, how beneficial are your thoughts? Do these thoughts help you or do they upset you? How do they make you feel? What thoughts are inaccurate assumptions that you can work on to change? Is this how you want to feel? How can you think to feel differently?

If you believe limiting beliefs you create yourself a life of limitations. It is your own disbeliefs that don't allow you to live a life of total love. It is so important to become aware of your inner chatter. You will notice that it is impossible to try to force the mind to stop buzzing. As soon as you try to force the thoughts a conflict arises. The way out of the mind jumble of thoughts is to find the space where silence is, through meditation, mindfulness, yoga, alternative rituals like singing, painting, dancing, walks in nature.

To change you thoughts means to question them and replace those that do not benefit you.

Train yourself to see something good in everything - If you change your thoughts, you change the perception of who you are, your words, your actions, your experiences and your life will change. You are what you think - let your life be filled with colors of love, compassion and acceptance. Everyday when you wake up choose positive thoughts! Play some music, choose clothes with colors, anything that can help you change your mood.

Fear versus Love

I believe that everything in life is origin from love or from fear. You can love life, or be afraid of life. You can feel love in your relationship, or you can be afraid of being left/abandoned/wounded etc. The choice is yours. I believe in the power of thought and that what you believe in is growing and becoming a self-fulfilling prophecy. If you have a strong belief that you will be hurt, chances are that you will be hurt. If you love yourself and believe that others will love you chances are that others will love you. Of course, sometimes it happens that some do not love you the way you desire but that does not make you a less loving and valuable creature. Maybe it is just not meant to be. Need it be more complicated than that? It is your approach to how you deal with what is happening around you which decides how you feel and if you want to look at life with loving eyes, or with fear in your eyes. To control, always wanting to be right, being jealous, manipulating etc is not love - its fear and fear comes from a poor self-confidence that origin from misguided thoughts and beliefs.

If you fall instantly in love with someone that you've never met before, you know nothing about that person. You fall in love with what you see and what you feel. You have no real knowledge of the person in question. If you spend time with the person you get more and more knowledge about him/her. You create a picture of how he/she is based on how much fear and love you carry in yourself. You get ideas and expectations about the persons persona based on your previous experience. The more fears you carry the more distorted the picture of the person you have met in a positive or negative sense. The more fear, the more interpretations. The truth might be close to what you have interpreted, but it might as well be very far away. If you fall in love with someone that you know, you have a reasonably good idea of who the other person is. But your love it is still based on how much fear you have in your back pack, the more fear the more distorted picture.

You are very much affected by what you yourself bring into your relations. If you bring fear, judgmental, prejudice, preconceptions, projections and if you do not talk about how you feel, show who you are or what you expect, it is very likely that you think you have fallen in love and then it turns out to be something other than what you expected. As a child you wanted to feel safe and loved especially by your guardians. If you grow up in a home where there for an example was chaos and fear, where there were fights, infidelity, where you could not express yourself, you felt alone, abandoned or other things that strongly affected you, you will automatically connect these feelings with love. Because you assume that this is the way you show love. This is how love should be felt. Then it becomes natural that you seek the same emotional situations that you recognize as familiar. When you go out to find a partner, it is your subconscious that is in control. You may think that you want a partner who is reliable or stable and then you end up with someone who is mean and maybe on the verge of depression. The unconscious seeks what it lacks and recognize.

If your upbringing is marked by dysfunctional patterns, there is a risk that you have a mistaken idea of what love really is and need to redefine the concept. I had a client for quite some time and we worked with her upbringing patterns. She always managed to fall for the same kind of men that always proved to be quite unreliable. Finally it was time for her to challenge herself to meet someone who was completely different from the ones she used to go on dates with. A year later she came back and was completely shocked by the experience of having a relationship with the man she had met. He is confident, open, and he actually cares about me she told me absolutely radiant. I thought that relationships mattered drama and that quarrel should always be included, but this is completely different. I feel completely calm, is this love? To fall in love with someone is often quite easy but to recognize true love is not always as obvious. It is important to know the difference between being in love with someone and loving someone. To be in love with someone is initially more of attraction than to love someone. Love is characterized by a willingness to give unconditionally and to do that you need to behave authentically. Love makes you feel safe.

When you encounter something that you are afraid of, you frequently try to change it. You may get angry or irritated instead of accepting. It's pretty easy to think and say things like, if he only, if she was this way instead. This way of handling fear is creating an internal resistance in you. If you have resistance in a conflict you do not listen fully to what is said, instead you try to handle the situation so that it will suit you. If you choose to surrender to your fear and release your expectations, take a deep breath, open your heart and listen, listen without defence and without resistance. Then you receive the information that you receive, no more no less, you give the other party the opportunity to own their feelings and opinions and let them be heard and to be confirmed. This is love. If you go into defence, it is fear that is talking and you want to have control. If you give up the idea that it is you who is right and the belief that you know what will be said in the next step and instead concentrate on listening, you are not only giving love a chance, you give both of you a change to evolve.

When you are in a relationship with someone, it will inevitably sometimes create feelings or behaviours from the other party that does not fit into your picture of how you want it to be. Every time your partner says/does something that you feel is inappropriate it may provoke feelings of anger or resentment within you. Your task is to turn inward.

What are you afraid of? To not be loved, not being good enough, to be left, to not be heard, or not to be seen? It is constantly a conscious choice to change these thoughts. What you think about your self, you feel.

If you assume that other people do not want to hurt you it becomes a little easier. If you choose to believe that people are doing things out of love or fear, it's pretty easy to see that nasty, harmful comments are based on fear. And if you instead of meeting fear with fear, face fear with love the situation becomes different. It does not mean that you accept, it just means that you are secure enough in yourself to realize that the person facing you are very scared, and that it is basically not about you. Once you learn how to enter and to trust that it is you who create the feeling and not someone else who make you feel bad, you learn to live a more loving life and you learn to trust that it is you who chooses how much love you want to experience.

If you practice loving yourself you find love easier and easier every time. You feel more present and you feel the power within you. When you can feel this, you are not dependent on someone else to fill your voids. With that said, it's not meant for you to abstain from relationships, only that you can let go of all expectations of perfect love from someone else. When you feel that you can accept others for who they are and dare to show yourself openly and honestly, you can see all your relations in a clearer light.

It is possible to work with your fears and use them to your advantage. Fear contains powerful messages. When you are brave enough to be with what scares you, you can create a new path for healing. No matter what you're worried about do not judge your fears but invite them as your teacher.

It is common to belittle your fears and pretend that they do not exist. To be afraid, means that you are outside of your comfort zone and here you have the choice to do something that can make you expand. Fear is one of the many colours in your emotional palette, and its here for a reason and that reason causes change. It is no weakness to be afraid. And guess what, you're not alone. We are all more or less afraid, in any case, very few people are completely fearless.

So what do you do when you get scared? How can you get answers out of your fears without them dragging you down? Take yourself back to the present moment. Here and now. Feel the earth beneath your feet, look around. This is reality. This is for real. This is what is happening right now. Open your heart, feel the emotions fluttering in your stomach. You should not fight against your fear, if you resist it leads to panic, just sit with it. Have faith that your feelings will help you. Breathe in through your nose, exhale through your mouth. Take deep and slow breath. Have the courage to stay in the feeling. If there are feelings of sadness, let them be there. If anger comes up, it is also okay. This is the mature way, this is the responsible place to be. When you are ready, start listening to what message your feelings bring. Get in touch with what comes up. Do not stress. Let your fear speak. Take the time to listen.

Do a "check up" on how it feels in your stomach. Is your fear constructive or is it destructive? If you agree with your fear, begin to explore why you agree and how you can make a healthy change to stop believing in negative thoughts. Do you need help to create a new pattern of thoughts and feelings? If you do not agree with the feeling of fear, you can simply tell it that you do not intend to react or respond to it. This immediately creates a new thought and a new behaviour. If you can not change your patterns by yourself, get some professional help because it is so unnecessary to have unwanted feelings that doesn't allow you to live your life to the fully.

Another way to get back into your body and into the present moment is through movement. When you activate your body it is changing your perspective. A walk, a bike ride, dance, whatever suits you can make you see more clearly what you are feeling. But beware that you do not use any of these options as an escape rather than facing what you are afraid of.

Love is greater than fear. And love is everywhere, it may hide but it is everywhere. Love and acceptance is a good way to calm a troubled soul. Affirmations are another way to dealing with fear. To say words that give you a soothing effect and again shift the focus from what you are afraid of to positive messages can give you stress reduction. "Although I'm really scared, I love and accept myself". Loss of control usually creates more fear it might be many unpleasant changes taking place at the same time in your life? It can be changes in your relationship, at work, new events or a lot of new information to take in. Give yourself a break. You are human. One trick is to stop being so critical, accept and learn from all aspects of yourself. Anxiety is often scary and cause symptoms that reinforce your fear. To repress feelings in a panic attack often create a stronger sense of anxiety. The only way to be free from anxiety is to face the fear that lies beneath it.

Fear reduces when you focus on something that you are grateful for. Gratitude is a form of positive energy. If you want to feel the positive form from the energy of gratitude, you have to seek it. It does not arise by itself. By emphasizing gratitude instead of problems you replace negative thoughts with positive vibrations. Write down what you are grateful for, so you strengthen your sense of gratitude. Journaling can give you a new perspective on what is important to you and what you truly appreciate. Create a small ceremony before you go to sleep and think of the day's event and what you are grateful for. And remember the law of attraction. Be grateful for all the good things, and in return life provides you with more things to be grateful for. Often you devote your time to focus on what you do not have instead of what you actually have. Create your own attitude for finding gratitude.

When fear has a tight grasp on you, the worst thing you can do is try to escape. Challenge your fear! Dare to let it wash over you and you will discover that the feeling disappears faster? The more you dare to face, the less grip on your life it will have.

Avoid absorbing and taking in other people's fears. Distance yourself from the source of the negative; avoid having energy thieves in your immediate closeness. It does not mean you have to avoid all people carrying fear. It means that you need to make sure you are not taking in other people's fear in to your system. Realize that someone else's problem is not your problem and don't help to spread fear (in the form of gossip, comments, phobias, anxiety, etc.). Try sending loving energy into your heart, breathe in peace and breathe out fear.

> Ask yourself;
> What am I afraid of?
> What do I react to?
> What will happen if I surrender to the situation/ fear?
> What do I gain by sticking to fear? There is always a personal gain by sticking to something that you are afraid of?
> What obstacles must I remove before I surrender to fear?
> What's the worst scenario that can happen?

Create your own space in life where you can refill your love depots. Take a moment and think about what you need to create more love in your life. Do you need peace and quiet, more outdoor exercise, perhaps alone time? Find situations that give you feelings of joy, fill your home with things that give you smiles. Clear away anything that steals energy from you in the form of relationships that do not benefit you, things that just creates dust. A bouquet of flowers on the table can do wonders. Clear your mind and space and fill your life with love goals.

Trust

You build trust or you trust someone based on your previous experiences. You can make an active choice and choose to trust a person. Trust is something that many of us have a hard time with. As a child, you might learn that what your guardians say matches with what they actually deliver, and you learn that you can trust others around you. But sometimes it is enough that one guardian stands before you and tell you that everything is fine when you can feel that it is actually not true. When you lose faith in your own system, your ability to feel what is right or wrong you stop believing in your feelings and in yourself. You can also have guardians who repeatedly promise things they can not keep, so that the next time they give you a promise, you become immediately suspicious and do not trust that they will keep that promise. Tomorrow we will go on a picnic, we do it later, we buy it tomorrow - and none of this happens. Many of these "wounds" occurs when you are young, and when you are a child small "betrayal" feels like a big betrayal. You could not put the betrayal in relation to something else, because your world was pretty narrow. Separations and deaths can also be perceived as a major betrayal that creates trust issues. When a person has left you, it can create feelings like, I'm not good enough, I'm not worthy, I am always going to be alone, someone will always leave me and you lose faith in yourself and to others.

All of these wounds exist within you when you in adulthood go into relationships. You have unconsciously programmed yourself with "wounds" that launch when you're with others. That's why you need to pay attention to what kind of reactions goes on in yourself when you react and act on what anyone else says or does. You need to find out where the wounds are from and heal them so that you no longer respond/act because it hurts in you. A good way to challenge this fears, is to once again stand firm when it hurts, and to share with someone what is scary to get past the experience. What is it that makes you want to escape, what is it that makes you put up all these protective walls when someone says/does in a certain way?

How will you be able to enjoy real intimacy if you always push people away and not let them come close? How will you enjoy a relationship if you do not dare to be honest and have faith?

For it to be a good relationship you have to have the courage to trust. You need to choose faith. You might meet a rejection or betrayal now and then, but if you have a positive attitude, it helps you so much more. You get loving encounters, beautiful experiences and priceless memories. Personally, I know that I sometimes have trust issues but I also challenged them to be something that I can immediately recognition and pronounce if they occur. Today, I meet people and can immediately have confidence in them, something that was unthinkable before. You can not teach an old dog to sit, is a Swedish saying that is not true. Anyone can make an active choice to change their mind if they are willing. And with that choice, we are also willing to let love in.

Do you trust your partner?
Do you trust your family?
Do you trust your friends?
Do you trust yourself?
If not, why?

Feminine and Masculine

It is for me a big difference between being feminine and being a female. When we talk about feminine and masculine we often talk about this in terms of what we call the culturally defined gender roles and stereotypes, and the value they are attributed. We usually create our society after the norm of what most people think is right or wrong. This standard changes with time and in different cultures, depending on what we accept and not accept. And we all know that for a very long time the Western world has lived with a male-dominated norm. The masculine characteristics have been valued as higher then the feminine even do both man and woman consists of both masculine and feminine.

We have gone from that the old goddess tradition was the highest valued norm to woman being subservient to the masculine characteristics. And perhaps that was what was needed at that time to be able to get the progress and evolution forward. Over time, women have freed themselves and wanting to be valued equally. Today, the woman's economic and social conditions are better than ever (although on many levels there is still much to do). But the question is, if parts of the female liberation are at the expense of oppressing feminine characteristics? I'll explain what I mean. And to do that, we start by looking at what it is that separates the masculine and the feminine characteristics, it is quite significant for how we react and act in relations to each other.

When I say that there is a difference between being feminine and to be a woman, I mean our essence, our unique qualities, our innermost being. For me, a woman may be incredibly much a female but not feminine. Many women have added so many of the male characteristics so the feminine side has been pushed away or hidden. This is often done unconsciously.

There are biological and psychological differences between men and women. The way we think, feel and act are not always the same. Women are controlled by the right brain (intuitive) while men are controlled by the left (logical). Cooperation between the masculine and feminine sides in the individual is the basis for all creation. And we need to develop both these sides of ourselves to live as harmoniously as possible. Both sides have an equal value and we need to take advantage of the differences.

The most distinctive differences between the feminine and the masculine qualities that I write about are those that history has shown to have the greatest impact on the way we act and react. Of course this is not 100% true because we are all individuals. But it is possible to see a fairly clear pattern. And it is also important to remember that we all need our feminine and masculine characteristics in order to function optimally. The need is always a duality.

Feminine characteristics, intuitive, emotional, nurturing, networking, holistic perspective - family, health, work, includes everyone in decisions. The feminine often communicates in circular. Start talking about one thing and talk around to get to the core/result. We often talk about a problem but don't want the partner to solve the problem, it's all about the partner listening, which is a form to get close and create intimacy. As the masculine the best thing you can do is to meet the feminine in the feeling, it's not often about the problem. Don't start fixing and try to find solutions without asking first.

Masculine characteristics, handling, intellectually, power, logic, action, independence, competition, objectives, performance, takes decisions alone. The masculine often communicates from A to B, a very straight, linear communication. For a feminine the best thing you can do is not to add another value to what is being said than what has just been said. Do not create your own interpretation and expectations.

Of course there are a lot more differences between the feminine and the masculine. You must bear me with on the words her and him in the text, she will represent the feminine and the masculine is he.

The feminine wants to be listened to, but not be told what to do. She also has an ability to interpret him wrong because the masculine often shows his love by doing. The masculine on his part has difficulties to know what to do with what she says, because he is trying to sort the circular maze of words and find out what it is that is important.

The masculine is often trying to make sure that his family is taken care of by doing. He often does it in terms of work and to fix things at home. The female has a greater need of emotional support in the form of someone physically there. In relationship is also easy to believe that the other partner should know what you feel and think but there are many times this is not the case. The masculine perceive many times that the feminine is nagging and he think that she is bothersome. He also often feels that when he tries to take charge, he will only be criticized.

The feminine feel that was the masculine perceive as nagging is very clear. So clear that when the female has had enough and leaves him the masculine won't understand why. He has only heard the nagging of words. The feminine believe that the masculine has listened and understood everything and know why she leaves.

The feminine get angry and disappointed, she complains about things in an emotional way but get no response. He can not find the logic in her words and it doesn't matter how he responds to it, because it is perceived as the wrong answer. So he pulls away instead and she feels no involvement from his part. You need to pay attention to how you as an individual and as a couple communicate. Does your partner really understand what you say and what you really mean? I have always thought that the clarity of asking my partner to confirm that he has understood what I mean have been ridiculous. With time I have learned that it is much better to ask one extra time than to create unnecessary misunderstandings.

In today's culture (although it is starting to change) we have not learned to use the feminine and the masculine characteristics in a natural way and in the right proportion to each other. Today many women have learned to use the masculine characteristics and with it unconsciously denied and repressed a lot of their feminine qualities. It certainly has to do with the fact that women have had to adapt to a man's world that has been ruling in both the social and economic context. The masculine characteristics are still today the norm in the business world and are valued most highly. It has in no way been a conscious choice to let go and repress the feminine side. But you can not escape the fact that on many places in the world the feminine role is still submissive to the male role which gives power and it is in some men's interest to maintain that power. Similar dilemma also applies to the masculine characteristics. Woman's entries into the labor market and with equal conditions also have forced man to adapt. It is easy to feel confused about how to be and behave in order to be as good a masculine man as possible. Women have demanded that the man should be more feminine, while the masculine qualities are most valued by the norm. In the traditional male role men learns to deny and repress their feminine side and then came the women wanting them to appear more feminine. Media on the other hand creates a picture of men as uncontrollable and too much in their masculine energy.

The interesting thing that I often hear is that a woman who is very masculine in her way to be has difficulties with a man who is very feminine. She simply runs him over. She feels that she needs a man who is even stronger masculine than she is. Unfortunately, often these relationships lead to a power struggle in which it will be difficult for anyone to win. And a masculine man wants a feminine woman at his side, he does not want someone who specializes in the same behaviour as himself. This is something that we need to be aware of. It is clearly that there are some generalizations but there is also some truth in this. We need balance and we need to evaluate the feminine and the masculine characteristics as equal worth. It is not in our best interest to let women take over the masculine traits and live far way from her actual purpose. If she does the risk is high that she will get stress related illnesses. It is not for nothing that so many women drop out of the business world, opening yoga studios and choose an alternative career. And a lot of men start to feel lost and stressed by being insecure in the man role. It is difficult to find any obvious role models who are secure in their masculinity and femininity. And now we are at some kind of crossroads and we feel quite confused and many are very insecure in their roles in the partnership. If we try to compete and create equality by suppressing qualities it will lead to alienation, health problems and less evolution. We don't want power struggle in our relationships, we want the freedom to be our self.

The gender roles we have, tell us how we should conduct ourselves in order to fit in, get a promotion or attracting a partner. They tell us what is right or wrong and as a directly result we get a feeling that we need to change or hide any part of our personality. We adapt to other people's standards and we automatically take over as our own. Unfortunately, it will colour everything we see and meet around us. It colours our image of the perfect partner, limits us and creates great expectations of those we meet. The sad part is that the feminine characteristics have been suppressed more and more and that it is often women themselves who look down on these qualities. I talked about my own personal experience of suppressing my feminine side in a radio show. I used to be very good at looking down on many feminine qualities, and thinking of them as a weakness. Then I realized that I created my own emotional suffering because I was not living my own truth. When woman suppress the feminine side and replace these features makes men also at a greater degree look down on the feminine. Which, in the next step make a man afraid to use their feminine qualities? It becomes a self-fulfilling prophecy of projections to downgrade the feminine characteristics. It is sad and it is completely unnecessary when we instead can utilize the full spectrum of our emotions and open up the opportunity to become more authentic.

The answer is not to suppress either the feminine or the masculine characteristics but to improve both to its rightful level. When both men and women are brave enough to balance the feminine and the masculine within themselves, we can make the world a much better place. Your future lies in embracing your feelings, your vulnerability, your intuition, your solidarity and to love each other with an open heart without fear. You can only do these if you dare to live in line with yourself without looking at what others do and what they think about you.

Since all changes always begin in yourself this is where you need to start.

> How do you feel about your masculine and feminine qualities?
> Are some qualities worth more than the other? Why?
> What does it mean to you in your everyday life?
> Are you suppressing qualities that you actually would like to show?
> What do you need to change to be true to yourself?

Becoming aware of the genetic differences and the cultural prejudices and what norm you use allows you to quickly see whatever it is you do to help increase or decrease the differences.

What can you do to evaluate the masculine and feminine characteristics as equal? It is not about standing on the barricade and proclaims what is right or wrong but just to observe how it works in everyday life and what you can change and what you want to contribute with.

And above all, how true and honest are you against yourself? Can you express your genuine you the way that you really want, or are you trying to fit in?

Intuition

Have you been taught not to trust your inner voice, not to express yourself honestly and truthfully? Maybe you have learned how you should behave and be, and what was expected of you? You were born as an innocent child in need of closeness, security and food. Unfortunately, you needed very little to start doubting your intuition, the gut feeling that tells you what is right or wrong.

It's enough for a sad or angry caretaker to stand in front of you saying that everything is fine, but you know with your whole body that this is not true and you start to doubt your own ability to trust your feelings. If you are the authority standing in front of a small child and tell the child that he/she's senses is wrong the child will eventually believe it. When you consistently shut down your intuitive knowledge and listen to authority figures, you lose your confidence in yourself. You start to question how you yourself feel and repress your feelings. You may also feel that the person, who tells you direct or indirect that you're feelings are wrong, is not really interested in you and your answers. When you feel that your intuition is not heard you often start to respond to others with the word "good or fine." When you have responded "good or fine" to the same question a number of times you also silences down your intuition. But your intuition is somewhere in there wanting to be awakened.

Your intuition can not be wrong. Intuition is your wake up call, your system's way to wake you up and say to you that you are on the right or wrong track. But the question is can you hear it? Do you listen to it? I think you are much better at hearing and feeling your intuition than you think you are. In a relationship, you know that something is wrong but you can not quite put a finger on it. A feeling, you know? You may be afraid of losing a partner or to appear as controlling or jealous so you silences your gut feelings and pretend that everything is fine. Many of us have in one way or another programmed our minds to doubt intuition.

Some people start questioning right away when they have a feeling that something is not right. To get confirmation that the intuition is right strengthens your trust in it. If someone instead is lying to you when you ask a question and your gut instinct tells you that something is wrong creates a greater chaos in your system than to hear the truth. This is a fact many clients testify about. A truth you can do something about, you can take a decision. A lie when your system says otherwise creates trust problems that will be difficult to repair. It also means that you rely much less on your own system. And if you do not trust your system you will not trust someone else's. This leads to a feeling of emptiness, helplessness, and that there is no point. You need to trust your inner truths and you need to learn to follow your own voice.

It is an art to learn to trust your intuition, you have so many other voices that speak to you. Your intellect has its programming with doubts and fears. Other people have opinions, you have a conscience that often tells you to be a kind good person, and how you should and should not do/

be, and you are accustomed to adapt. Have you ever said, I can not do this, what will others say, what a ridiculous idea? There are so many models of explanation and excuses for you to not listen to your intuition. But there is an even greater disadvantage not to listen and live by your intuition. You then live in a false security, and with a lot of fear. You are not true to yourself, and you do not live the way your soul really wants to live, and it creates stress in your body. If you don't feel that you are in harmony then how can your relationships be harmonious? The strength lies in living in harmony with your own power.

If you learn to listen, you will discover that you can use your intuition and it can help you create integrity that protects you from external influences.

What can you do when your world feels like chaos and you do not know what's what? It is your true inner feelings or is it your logical thinking that has taken over and is talking to you?

I usually see the logic as a camera lens, a lens that is unique to me. Through this lens, I get pure information into my brain. I immediately start analyzing. I am coloured by past experiences of what is right or wrong in my life. Then I start to filter the information and interpret it. I'm generalizing, I exclude parts of the information, I may interpret it as not important or I interpret parts that are extra important. In other words, I distort it. When I am finished with my "analysis" it does not look as the information did when it came into the lens. How can I make the right decision after all these interpretations? Can you trust your logical thinking when it comes to relationships? Yes, in some cases you should. If you logically know that the relationship is not good for you even though the heart says something else you should listen. Bad is always bad and bad tend to get worse if you don't do something about it.

Often when something feels wrong, your intuition is screaming and trying to make you pay attention. Unfortunately, you have learned not to listen or to ignore the voice. In most cases, when you enter into a new relationship that is not the best for you, there are warning signs.

Start by listening to how it feels when you are following your intuition. If you are on the right path, it should feel like everything is getting easier, you get more power, you have a flow. This feels good, it feels fun and you feel safe, secure and loved. If you go against your intuition, you are losing energy, you feel powerless or having very little energy. This is not funny. This makes me worried. I'm bored, anxious or nervous.

To follow your intuition and rely on yourself instead of listening to others can make big changes, even for those who are closest to you. It is not just you who is affected by your changes. When it comes to changing behaviour it is not always appreciated by your nearest and dearest. They usually want everything to be as it always has been. Sometimes you lose close friends and relations, but there will be new relationships that will strengthen you, relationships that will benefit you. It is important to remain in what feels right for you regardless of what others think. If you get rid of old baggage you can fill it with new experiences.

Try to do the opposite of what you normally do just to experience how it feels. Do you like anyone tell him/her, if you are attracted say it to the person of your interest, don't do and say things that doesn't feel right to you. We are often afraid to be rejected and we have learned not to behave in a certain way and we feel vulnerable when we cross our limits for how we usually behave. But it's worth it, you can not get more than a no, or that someone does not feel the same way as you do, but who cares? It is worth it to try new ways to be honest in your communication and true against your self.

> Can you remember a time when you have felt an
> answer in your body?

Can you remember a situation where you felt drawn to someone or something?

Try to practice moving past your intellect and listening to your inner heart.

When a situation occur, how does it feel? Do you feel expansive or contracted?

Attachment Theory

To make a change in your life, you can get a lot of help by looking at past patterns. Your past contributes to what you feel in your relationships. Attachment theory's author is John Bowlby (1907-1990) a British psychiatrist. Attachment theory is the result of 60 years of research and is based on the discovery that we humans learn to create relationships when we are very young. These skills, we take with us and use the rest of our lives. Attachment patterns are activated unconsciously in meetings with other people. Most of the times we act and react automatically without thinking or questioning were these reactions come from. Attachment theory explains why people experience love and relationships so different and why some people are drawn to each other and why it sometimes does not work as we have imagined. The emotional patterns that show when you enter into a new relationship are based on the experience you have had in the past. In the early stages of love, you do not notice to any appreciable extent your attachments, but once the first love phase has passed, the attachment related theory is starting to slowly show its true self. If any of you begins to withdraw, avoid conflict, always know best, etc. feelings of being misunderstood and abandoned are typical examples of early dysfunctional attachment patterns.

The attachment is intended to protect a child against future dangers that threaten the child's survival. Infants are born genetically programmed to develop related attachment to the people in its closeness. A child often has strong ties to between one and five people in its first year. Attachment is not about the child liking someone; it is about connecting with, develop and maintain the capacity to make use of certain people as a source of security and protection during moments where the child feels danger and threats. How you learn to relate to the people who are in your immediate environment from birth is usually the pattern that you follow for the rest of your life. This means that the quality of the relationship you once had for your parents or guardians (or absence of) plays an important role in how easy or difficult it is for you to create closeness to others. What is it that determines whether a child will develop a secure attachment or not?

Children with secure attachment have experience emotionally present parents/guardians. These are sensitive to the child's signals and predictable to how they react. This means that the child can trust that their parents are there when needed. The child has learned by experience that the parent is available. That he or she sees, hears, understands and wants to help the child. The experience makes the baby safe in order to switch between exploring the world and seek refuge in the parent. It also gives the child a confidence in their own ability to be with others, and it is something that is meant to create patterns for future intimate relationships.

Children who do not have a secure attachment to their parent/guardian have rather more experience of the parent reacting negatively, erratically or not at all on the child when they express their emotional needs. This gives an insecure child that easily becomes unsure of him/her and will bring this pattern in future relationships.

As a child you had no ability to analyze what was right or wrong, so it is no wonder that these truths that you experienced is deeply rooted in your soul. By really looking at your attachments you will find many "truths" that you actually no longer benefit from today, but rather make it difficult for you in your relationships. All people have "wounds" in their attachment patterns. It does not mean that all parents/guardians have been "bad or wrong". However, by watching your wounds you can get a much better understanding of why you react and act like you do in relationships. Gaining insight allows you to challenge yourself to do differently next time something happens that triggers your wounds.

All people belong to one of the four related groups;

Secure attachment
Confident children trust that the parent/guardian is trying to help the child in difficult or frightening situations.

As an adult, it's easy for you to get close to other people, but you also thrive well in your private company. You feel that connecting with others is easy and you make it work in the long term relationships and you do not experience loneliness as a threat. A secure attachment is based on trust. Security related context means that you as a child trusted that your parent was there and was protective. Children who know they can trust that their parent is predictable and responsive to the child's signals will also get a confidence in their own ability to interact and socialize with others. The fact that a child has a secure attachment does not mean that the child never experience fear or feel uneasy. These feelings are completely natural and also very important. In a relationship a secure attachments motives for having sex is to have intimacy, closeness and physical pleasure.

Insecure avoidant attachment

Children with insecure avoidant attachment have parents/guardians that are not ready or willing to meet the child's needs for closeness and security. The child learns, therefore to push away his need for closeness and appears instead as very independent.

As a child with insecure avoidance related pattern you expect to be alienated and rejected when you need help. You learn early not to seek closeness and support, but rather handle yourself. You often try to think your way to answers rather than to feel the answer. If you relate to insecure avoidant you are very social and loved and work well in superficial relationships. You are good at "taking people" and are popular in your social environment. But in close relationships you keep a distance. You may be difficult to get into life and you often take a step back when experiencing closeness. You may be told that you are too perfect. In relationships you build up a certain closeness but the feeling is still of having something to lose. You want to get close but the attachment says what it has always said, that the other person is not ready or willing to meet your desire. Your feelings may not be seen outwardly, for it will lead to you being turned away again, so instead you increase the distance. The insecure avoiding attachment also says that other people close to you do not want to see your expectations and your needs. So you hide your needs and adapt after your partner instead. There is a risk that your partner leaves you because they never get to know you. An insecure avoiding attachment motives for having sex are to secure the relationship.

Ambivalent attachment

If you have an ambivalent tie you experienced a parent/guardian who had an unpredictable behaviour. As a child, you did never now how your parents would react. Sometimes they cared and sometimes you were rejected when seeking help and comfort. The uncertainty made you feel separation, anxiety and fear. You were very emotionally driven as a child.

As adult you are perceived often as creative and close to your feelings. You have easy to bid on yourself. In relationships, opposed to the insecure avoiding - you like to get close to people. The problem may be that you sometimes want more than what others are willing to give. Your strong desire for closeness can scare others. The back of the coin could be that you are so afraid of being abandoned so instead you avoid close relationships. As an ambivalent you are often worried about being abandoned. In relationships, the feeling often is that people can love you, but chances are that they change and disappear. In a new relationship many testify that they feel good together with the partner, but as soon as they are alone they feel abandoned and useless. The only thing that can calm is to contact the partner, to get as close as possible, it means that the person is often seen as clingy. The sexual desire is linked to the fear of being rejected. The desire increases before a separation or risk of rejection. The motive for having sex is to feel closeness, manage their emotions to prevent anxiety and to get a feeling of being taken care of.

Disoriented/disorganized attachment
A child with disoriented attachment has had parents/guardians who were threatening and unpredictable. This attachment patterns often develop in children who grow up with physical or mental abuse or with parents who have difficult experiences from their own childhood that makes them unable to interpret their child's signals correctly. Parents that can become angry or fearful when the child expresses their feelings; the child feels that the parent is tough and scary. The child then develops a vision of the parent as dangerous and the child also receives a vision of himself as frightening.

Disoriented is based on fear. As a child you have a need for closeness, comfort and protection, but in contact with your parent you could demonstrate behaviours, like hiding behind a chair, go with your back against the parent, holding hands for your face (as a guard) at the sight of the parent. The reason for this is that as a child your attachments were to the same person who raised your fear. A child may be worried or frightened by something in their environment and needing closeness from a parent/guardian who with his/her behaviour reinforces the need for protection. But who should the child turn to? There is no one else.

In attachment, the connection causes the child to the arms of their parents, which makes the child get closer to the scary parents. The child ends up in an impossible conflict. As an uncertain, disoriented person, you are often perceived as confident and determine. You are often boundless in your new contacts and often have strong controlling relationships that contain very little closeness. You often experience a threat in the relationship, and often choose a completely harmless partner. You are often boundless in your sexuality and often agree on things you do not really want. You have relationships without sex or relationship based solely on sex. You really have no motive for having sex.

Summary;
A person with secure attachment has an image of other people as available and compassionate. If you feel trust or stress you move further in the relationships.

If you have an insecure avoidant attachment you often have a picture of other people as resistant or too intrusive. In relationships at both closeness and stress you keep the distance or adapts exaggerated.

As a person with ambivalent attachment you have a picture of other people as fickle and unpredictable. In relationships at both closeness and stress you become alternately clingy or distancing.

As a person with disoriented attachment you may have a picture of other people as repellent and frightening. In relationships, you want control.

How can you change your attachment patterns? All changes begin with awareness. Becoming aware of what governs you and what you have with you from the past. Look at the different attachment patterns, which one feels most familiar to you. Notice how you relate to other people, especially in your close relationships. What is it that you fall for in a particular person? How do you feel in your relationship? Can you see the patterns from your upbringing? Ask your partner, friends or family how they perceive you. Do they experience you as secure, distancing, clingy, or jealous?

If you want to change your behaviour set up small milestones that you think you can achieve. If you keep other people on distance, decide to tell something personal to someone. If you scare off others with your closeness start paying attention to when and why, and try not to. Try to do things contrary to what you usually do. Be aware of your emotional reactions when you try to do something different. It may arouse some fear and in some cases, the discomfort can be very strong, but it is not dangerous and it is by challenging your fears that you learn to create new patterns.

Change occurs through new experiences that provide new models and alter your own attachment. Thoughts and intellect do not bite on your emotional memory, but by challenging your fear by doing differently you can get so much better relationships. By meeting a different personality type than you usually do helps you heal from your wounds. If an unsafe meet a secure attachment and the secure attachment stays, and shows that it can be trusted, slowly a new pattern is created. Do the opposite - act contrary to what you perceive as safe for you.

Now you have read a little on attachment theory, and hopefully you have found something that you recognize or may have felt as an Aha experience. You may have find an answer to why you are the one who leaves first, why you avoid confrontations, why you are uncomfortable or anything else that might be of use to you. Gain knowledge and become aware.

To read more about attachment theory;
A Secure Base, Bowlby John

Purpose

What do you want to get out of your relationship? I always talk a lot about purpose, that the purpose must be right. This also applies in a relationship. Some people have a very clear purpose before they go into a relationship. It may be that you want to start a family, you want someone to share your life with, to share interests or you just want to have a sexual relationship. The important thing is that both parties should agree on the purpose. A purpose need not be anything fancy; it can be anything from having a family, to have someone to have fun with, to plan for retirement, a common interest, etc. But it is important as soon as you feel that your purpose with the relationship begins to change, tell this to your other half. If you have agreed on something and all of a sudden the situation is completely different, maybe you should give the other person a chance to change with you (if that is what you want). Be honest and say what you feel and what you would like to do, and then you will decide whether you should follow each other on a new path or if you should go on different roads. Make your intentions clear.

If you choose to make a long journey of life together it is often different purposes in different stages of life. The first infatuation might have fun period changing into a family project, then suddenly changing again when the kids move out and you struggle to find a way back to being just a couple again etc. How to find a meaning and a context will help you coping with changes.

To have a purpose gives a higher meaning, something to strive for giving you a larger sense of belonging together. If you do not have a purpose it can feel like you are living from day to day and you do not really know where you are going. Some people use the reasons, I do not want to be alone or I need someone to acknowledge me. I would not call this a loving relationship. Anytime you want something from another person, you get depended on the other person and to be dependent is no true love. If you can not handle being alone and are looking for another person to keep you company you do not take full responsibility for your own wellbeing. You want someone else to fix it for you. And if you need someone else to confirm you it shows that you do not love yourself, so you need someone else to do it. If you do not love yourself, how can you love someone else? This will inevitably involve dependency and manipulation to get what you want out of someone other than yourself. And you are not willing to take responsibility for your own life.

The purpose of a relationship is not primarily to be happy but to heal your wounds. Choose love, be fearless and become honest and true. And then you will be happy because you start paying attention to what you contribute with, you stop thinking negative thoughts, you eliminate self-criticism and you begin to honour the quality of the unseen forces that hold yourself together.

How do you know when you are living your life purpose? When you feel that your present moments are perfect. When you think this is exactly where you want to be right now. Nothing could be more perfect than this. Joy here and now, not yesterday and not tomorrow. The feeling is the result of total acceptance of the present. An inner peace is close to joy, and then you can be fairly neutral somewhere in the middle of your emotional state. Far away from joy is anger and even farther away is fear. Choose consciously the option that gives you the most joy and happiness in your everyday life.

> What is the purpose with your/a relationship?
> What do you want to accomplish and feel?

Values

Some of you have a very clear idea about what your values are, what you think is important and how you perceive tings. A value is often something that affects you very deeply. Something that you feel is very important, examples of this can be political values, questions about religion, infidelity, abortion. A value often gives a quick, deep, crystal clear answer. It encourages you to do what is right for you. Values govern your choices in life. They can touch you very deeply emotionally, they affect your behaviour and they affect how you act in different situations.

The problem as I see it with values is that we often have them handed down for generations. So are you really sure that they are your own values? There can be a big difference on how you live your life and how you want to live your life. You learn as very young what is right or wrong from your guardians and the community - the current norm. You may get into your teens, and get values by peer pressure or because you want to belong to a particular social structure. Most often, you do not think about what values you have, they exist in the background and will automatically show themselves if someone asks the right question, or when you have a strong sense of right or wrong. If you start reviewing your values at depth, it is not at all certain that you still feel the same way. Maybe you've outgrown your values and recognize that you have changed how you perceive life or what you feel about a particular question. For some couples, it works very well to live with someone who has completely different values. For others, it will not work at all.

Values are fun to explore, to ask yourself questions like what do I stand for, what is important to me? Are my values based on material wealth or personal well-being? Can I imagine being with a man/woman who thinks in a certain way that is not consistent with how I feel?

It is important to know what values you have, if you do not know, how will anyone else know? They also give your life meaning and motivation. They help you with your priorities in life. I am absolutely certain that how you live according to your values affects your health.

> What is important to you?
> Do you live accordingly to your values?
> How do your values fit into your relationship?
> Do you have similar or different values?
> If you are not in a relationship but want to be, is there something that is a must have or something that is unthinkable?

Needs

What needs are satisfied in your relationship? What is a necessity for you? Security, sleep, sex, closeness, intimacy, progress, creativity, freedom? Why do you want to have freedom while you're in a relationship someone said a little sarcastically to me? It depends on how you define the word freedom. For me freedom is equal to love. Freedom exists only when love is present. It's vital that my partner trust me and do not have to control me. I want to enjoy my own time without feeling guilty for it. And I want to give the same freedom to my partner. It is easy to fall into thoughts like, if my partner is independent I will no longer be needed. Freedom is not the opposite from having a serious relationship. A true relationship is based on love and in true love there is always freedom.

The feeling that someone is present to us is one of our greatest needs. But there is a big difference between being available and being fully present. Being present means that you give your partner full attention and really listen. No cooking, watching TV, fiddling with the phone, not doing other things at the same time. Make and take time to really listen to each other. It doesn't need to be such a long time each day when you actually pay attention and listen to each other. If you are not present for each other; you get a feeling of not being heard or seen and you have less chance to develop in the relationship. Being present is fundamental to how you are feeling in the relationship.

Creativity

I think most of us have a creative side that needs to be expressed. Many people like to write, sing, paint, dance and do some woodwork, baking, cooking, gardening or whatever it may be. All your hobbies (or work) that expresses colour, shape, and sound make you happier and more harmonious. It is important that both partners in a relationship make time for their hobbies. Anything that gives you joy is reflected in your relationship.

Development

You automatically evolve if you dare to look at your fears and challenge yourself. When you dare to question and be questioned. When you choose to have an open mind, be curios and learn as much as possible without judging. The problem with relationships is that we sometimes growth in different directions or at uneven pace. I personally think the whole idea of having relationships is to learn to evolve. But sometimes you come to the conclusion that in this relationship, you have learned enough, and it's time to move on. Don't see it as a failure, but only as a next step. By that I don't mean to just give up, but when it really is nothing more to learn, it is perhaps time to move on? Or maybe you decide that you are satisfied with what you have, and stay where you are.

Sleep

Maybe it sounds strange to write about sleeping in a book about relations but I have heard so many who get their sleep disturbed by their partner and do not want/dare to tackle the problem. And I'm not primarily talking about a snoring partner (who can get help). I'm talking about other distractions. This can involve anything from one of you need the light to be off and the other on, audio, televisions, children, no child in bed but also what you can and can not do during sleep. When it comes to sleep, I do not believe in compromises, you need all the recovery you can get and your sleep needs to feel safe and restful. If you need to have a cool or a warm room to sleep in, you should have it. It is extremely important that the intellect can retreat and the energy field around you need space. Your bedroom needs your restrictions, no one else's. Everyone is entitled to their sleep, sleep is vital. Solve all the problems that have to do with sleep. Make sure you get your sleep needs met so that you can wake up in a state of love.

Safety

To feel secure and safe is essential in a relationship, you would think, but unfortunately there are many relationships that do not have security. You choose relationships from what you experience as familiar and it gives you a feeling of safety. However, the security may be false if it is based on experiences that you actually fear. If you grew up in a family where the relationship have been a destructive one, it have created a lot of fear in you, but because it is something that you are used to, it also creates a sense of security. You recognize yourself, it becomes a normal state of mind for you. This is what we call the process of normalization. As you slowly get used to the destructive patterns in a relationship, it becomes normal. If you do not have any experience with this sort of pattern in a relationship you may have difficulties to understand this. That a person can stay in a negative relationship. But as we slowly get used to a particular pattern or approach it will become a normal condition in our daily lives. To have a good and fulfilling relationship genuine security not based on an underlying fear is a prerequisite.

> What needs do you want fulfilled in your relationship?
> Do you get these needs fulfilled?

If not, what can you do to fill your needs?

Do you know your partner needs?

How does it feel in your relationship, is there quality time where you are fully present and listen to each other without distractions?

If not, what can you do to incorporate this?

Self-esteem

Self-esteem or self-image is the definition you give yourself and how you perceive yourself right now. It is the description you give yourself when someone asks, or when you ask the question to yourself, who am I really? Self-esteem does not have anything to do with what you do, if you describe how good you are at what you do, you are talking about confidence. You can have a very high self confidence (think you are extremely good at what you do) and still have a very low self-esteem.

All good and less good qualities that you feel become your self-image. It is what you think is good and bad about yourself as a person that creates your feelings. Your self-esteem is constantly changing depending on your thoughts, and it needs to be replenished on a regular basis with more positive thoughts about yourself.

Most problems that arise in life come from a low self-esteem. You lack the security and love from yourself which makes you unconsciously or consciously insecure and afraid. You need to learn to love yourself. Again, the guardian and the important people in your upbringing helped and influenced your present self-image. As very young you mirrored yourself especially in the reactions you got from your parents, relatives, teachers, etc. In early age you lack the critical ability to objectively assess the reactions you got from your immediate environment. There and then was created what you perceive as good or bad characteristics.

You need to learn to act in line with how you define yourself. This means that if you see yourself as overweight or a smoker, you will be overweight or smoking. If you lose weight or stop smoking and continue to see yourself as overweight or smoking, the risk is higher that you will gain weight or start smoking again because it is the image that you have of yourself. Your behaviour and your thoughts have to be in tune with the image you have of yourself. If you think you are just going to initiate relationships with men/women who are not good for you, you will automatically find the men and women who are not good for you. It is the self-image you have given yourself. If you change your thoughts about yourself and make them more positive then your self esteem gets stronger and stronger.

If you change your self-image, you get more space to act differently. It gives you a better feeling and it gives you the courage to take you out of your comfort zone. You also get more opportunities to actually maintain the changes you are trying to implement in the form of weight loss, new exercise routines, quitting bad habits etc.

Your self-esteem can also be your greatest obstacle to change. Since self-esteem is so strongly associated with your comfort zone it can get you to back off or avoid things that make you feel insecure. It is often easier to say that it has always been like this, I can not change, or I have never done this before so I don't know how to. It is often easier and more comfortable to stick to old habits or stay in an old image of you.

Helena Källström

Since the self-image and self-esteem are so deeply rooted in childhood, it can be as I wrote before difficult to change. Every situation and every encounter you have had during your upbringing contributes to how strong your behaviour is today. If you repeatedly received negative confirmation of your behaviour it contributed to create a negative self-image. If you instead have received positive confirmation, it most likely gave you a stronger sense of self. Different situations caused deeper wounds than others.

Self-esteem is how you perceive yourself as a person. You need to realistically look at yourself and say this is me with weaknesses and shortcomings. Your weaknesses and your failures do not define you. A good self-esteem is to say that I am fine just as I am no more, no less. I take care of myself. I love myself. What you call failures is just obstacles to overcome to grow.

A good self-esteem means that you do not need to compare yourself with others, you run your own race whether it s about how you perform or how you look. You do not need someone else's confirmation that you are fine as you are. You should not glance at others and think that they are smarter or better looking. You are good as you are. You are doing the best you can for yourself. You believe in yourself. There is only one of you, how is it possible to compare yourself to someone else?

It is when you have a weak sense of self that you are influenced by what other people think about you. When you allow the opinions of others to make you feel bad. If you are sure that you are the best version of you and good enough as you are, you get confident in yourself and won't let yourself be influenced by others' opinions.

People who have a lot of opinions about you are those who have a poor self-esteem. When you allow your ego to take control of your mind, you often try to prove that you are better than other people. Bring your dark shadows (envy, jealousy etc) to light. Knowledge of self is the result of a process of self discovery. The more you discover and accept about your self the better self esteem. You are smarter because of your mistakes, you are stronger when you know how to handle your weakness.

With a good self-esteem, you feel loved in your mind, heart and your soul. With a good self-esteem, you can also receive love unconditionally. It is surprising how much compliments and encouragement that actually passes us by. You brush of gently and say, do you think this old cloth is stylish, it's very old, my hair, oh well, it looks as usual. The list goes on and on. And how often do we get compliments in intimate relationships and for some reason we minimize them even more, because we expect to hear them?

Why is this happening? Why do you have such a hard time receiving and accept the nice words that you get? Could it be that you only hear them but you don't feel it? You distrust if it is really true? He/she probably said this just to be nice? It does not feel real to you. Do you often in a relationship feel that you are the one giving? That you give and give but you get nothing back. Is this really true? Could it be that you actually get more back than you want to admit? Could it be that you are not able to receive? That you in secret criticize yourself so much that your response to the compliments that you get is a reflection of how hard you are on yourself?

But if you find it difficult to accept, how can you give? You can not give something you do not have? You react automatically to situations and to words that are spoken instead of in full awareness. And if you do not pay attention to how you think in these situations, the person giving you the kind compliments will eventually stop giving them. It is a fact, that we stop giving if the partner brushes of and behaves that he/she doesn't care.

To show love and appreciation to others can be a gateway to loving yourself. "You look nice!" "This food is amazing!" "You did great!" Do not be greedy, give out compliments and be sincere. Be delighted with others when they realize their dreams, "Oh this is fun", you look nice".

Positive comments also give you a love boost and we all need to be love bombed.

Self-esteem is to say yes to yourself no matter what happens, instead of sticking to an idea of how it should be or how you should behave.

Many times we have significantly more positive sides than we think about ourselves. Try to write down everything that you are good at and all your positive, good qualities. I think you will be amazed when you see how many there actually are.

You can not remove all your shortcomings, but you can change your automatically programming on how you think about yourself. What can you put in your plus bowl (things you are good at) which allows you to feel a sense of enough? The more you have on the plus side, the less you need to concern yourself with what you think are flaws. This way you do not take away what you perceive as negative, you only add to the plus side. When you have an imbalance in what you yourself think is positive and negative in your self-image your thoughts usually stick to the negative. And the negative sucks energy and it is increasing. Find your positive sides and when you focus on them they will grow. Do not believe in negative thoughts.

Some use affirmations when they practice on their self-esteem and for some, they work very well and for others not so well. For me it does not work, for the simple reason that I do not believe in what I'm saying. To stand in front of a mirror and repeat affirmations like "I love you" and do not believe the word does me no good. Again, the power of thought. You do not just have to think that you deserve the best, but you need to know, feel and believe in it. Without the emotional anchor the tank becomes empty words without meaning and there will be no change. Therefore, I personally feel that to add in the plus bowl is an easier way to get a change.

> What would you like to change about your
> self-esteem?
> How would you be and act if you choose another
> image?
> What do you need to add in your plus bowl?
> What qualities do you want to keep?
> If you think in negative terms, consider how you
> can turn your shadows into good qualities?

Being a bitch is an expression that occurs frequently in the Swedish society. There is a positive and a negative distinction of what we can add to the meaning. It could just as well mean something very negative as it can show a person with a huge strength, which we define as something positive. All characteristics that we think is negative, we can turn into our strength to love ourselves.

"Fake it until you make it" is also a good way to change the way we look at our self.

Finding examples of suitable characteristics in others and try to pretend what they feel and think about themselves can strengthen our own self image.

Another great way for you is to set aside a few minutes each night and write a diary with all the good qualities that you have appreciated in yourself during the day. At the beginning, they may feel like they are very few, but the more you practice the more positive side you will discover. Keep track of the good things in your life. Your thoughts affect your self-esteem, the choices you make, the actions you take, the lovers you choose, and the relationships you create. When you read a book like this it can be a lot of words that might feel like clichés but they are so true.

Confirmation

Confirmation is associated with your self esteem. If you have a low self-esteem you often seek confirmation from others. You are seeking acknowledgement that you are good enough, talented, smart, nice, competent, that you are the one etc. If you have enough self-esteem, you do not need to ask yourself these questions. Most people want to get some kind of confirmation and in particular with a partner. But searching for confirmation means you want approval that you are fine as you are. Then you let someone else rate you. You let someone else define your worth based on their values and their standards of what is right or wrong.

Should you really entrust that power to someone else? To seek external validation only provides you with temporary satisfaction.

Looking for confirmation? When and in what form, try to find situations where you become insecure and seeking confirmation?

How could you think instead?

What could you do instead to create another feeling?

To Take Things Personally

Just as in the beginning of the book with the example of the cashier, it's usually not about you when someone gets angry. You can be the trigger that your partner gets angry, but you are usually not the reason, it is not you that causes someone else's problem.

Let me give you an example.

I have a friend who can never keep time. And by never, I mean never, never ever. It's very frustrating when I'm always on time. I always have to wait and I already know in advance that I will have to wait, it will be postponed, and it will be prevented. There will be number of reasons. I used to be terribly annoyed to say the least. I could be annoyed long before because I knew there would be in my world, trouble. And if I did not just sulk and was annoyed, I could also go ahead and dwell on this so that we both became almost angry at each other.

I thought it was terribly disrespectful to me and my time and that I should be valued higher. And when I got angry, my poor friend was standing there wondering why I was so upset.

And yes, it could have been disrespectful to let me wait if this had been about me. It is not, it's about my friend who can not keep appointments. I thought my friend was quite hopeless and had a thousand things going on at once and could not handle it according to my standards.

I, in my turn if I'll be honest, was angry at myself because I thought that maybe this time we could be on time. I was angry and I was disappointed in myself that once again I had believed it would be different. I was angry because he did not value me higher, but honestly, who sat that value, me or my friend? I did it myself.

To take things personally is probably one of the biggest mistakes we make in life. We believe that everything is about us. How often do you not go around needlessly and are angry at what someone else has said or done to you. The person was rude to me, snarled, barked and treated me like I was less knowing, disrespectful, and unfair. The list goes on with all the wrongs someone can do to you.

> Why do you take it personally?
> What is the trigger in you?

If you have someone close to you who expresses themselves negatively against you, it does not sound like the person is feeling particularly well? So is it really about you? And the next question will be do you deserve to be treated this way? Maybe you think you do, but then I would advise you to go back in history and find out why you think you deserve this. For the decisions that you have taken about the feeling worthy, can be changed.

You need to take responsibility for your own feelings and you need to ask yourself, why you react? If it is not about you, why care so much? And what kind of relations do you want to have in your lives?

Communication

Communication is one of the most difficult things in a relationship no matter what kind of relationship it is. You often think that you are so good at expressing your self when you communicate but many times you are sadly, quite unclear. You also believe that your partner should know what you want, feel and like. Then you become moreover angry when he/she do not. Do you recognize yourself? I thought you knew what I wanted, you should know after all these years? You and your partner have different images of reality and it does not match the other's way of thinking, we all have different images based on different experiences.

You need to be better at expressing what you want and what you feel. A feeling can never be wrong. No one can ever take away from you what you feel. But how good are you at expressing your feelings? Are you telling when it's something you do not feel like doing? Or do you go along for the sake of domestic peace, because everyone else wants?

What is your responsibility in a communication process? Your responsibility is to get your message out in a way that is understandable to your partner, you are the one knowing what you want. But you also need to take responsibility for understanding your partner. All communication is verbal, tone and body posture. All your senses have to be present when listening – and be aware because there is a big difference between male and female communication. Women communicate in half with body language. Are you a man and standing with your back against your woman then you miss half of what she is saying and she will not feel heard. If the same question pops up again and again, who is it that does not listen and/or who is it that is not communicating clear enough?

When you try to impose on anyone your message, your opinions, your values, it is manipulation. If you think you are doing this with the other person's best interest in mind, I ask you to think again. You do not know how many times I have heard the words, I did it for your own good, and I did it because I care for you. If you do things (not asked for) for someone else, you deprive someone else their own responsibility to choose. And why do you believe that you have the authority to make a decision for someone else. Who gave you that permission?

When you get into situations and there is a conflict, the best way to start the conversation is with the words, I feel... Its better to express your feelings and what is happening within you, rather than with the words I want, I think, you ought to etc. This way you take responsibility for your feelings and the counterparty does not have to go in defence. The biggest cause of divorce is because we can not communicate and express our needs.

> Do you find it easy or difficult to communicate your message?
> How do you resolve conflicts?
> Does it work?
> If not, what can you do instead?

To Listened and To Be Heard

Do you listen to what the other person says with a closed heart (distracted, tired, scared etc)? If you do, you may miss how important this is for him/her, to be listened to is a way to be seen and to be affirmed on. As soon as you start thinking about dinner plans, things you forgot to do at work, doing other things at the same time, you simply are not there. Put away the book, turn off the TV, sit down and listen. You can not cheat your way through this. Everybody needs attention and it shows very clearly when someone is not listening. It's like having sex when someone's mind is drifting away, every cell in your body feels it.

Have you ever been going out on a date with someone who immediately takes up the phone and start watching/write messages, surf on social media and disappears into the mobile world while you're one on one? I'm not talking about being available to children or other important messages but rather as a bad habit and a need to be part of a digital world or the fear of missing something. Try sitting on the other side of the table and have a conversation when no one is looking you in the eye, and you do not know if that person is listening. It is rather difficult to remain in the sense of being seen and heard.

Listening also means not to add an interpretation of what is said. I want to have fun does not at all mean I want to have a family later. I do not want to commit myself, maybe not at all mean that you can change him/her later. I want to have sex may not mean at all that there may be a relationship. Do not let your values interpret to what is said to something other than what it actually is.

Your eyes are the mirror of the soul, and there are many eye gazing exercises that you can try to feel closer together and become more intimate in a relationship. You can communicate in silence or share your innermost thoughts. Take time to see each other in the eyes and concentrate on your breathing, then you can see beyond the physical body and personality. You get a deep contact beyond time and space that creates togetherness and a stronger bond. Sit relaxed and upright on chairs opposite each other but not so that you touch each other. Start with looking into each other's eyes for five minutes (when you have practiced a while, you can extend the time). Keep loving intentions and feel what is in the soul of the other person. When you become a little more experienced, you can start sharing your innermost thoughts and feelings, remember that when one person speaks, the other has to be quiet and listen.

> Do you dedicate time to talk and listen one on one?
> Are you good at actively listen without adding a different interpretation of what is said?
> Do you feel that your partner is listening to you?
> What can you do to make a change?

Forgiveness

To forgive is a process that you need to learn, and for some reason it gets easier as you get older (it might not be until then you have learned that life is too short to ponder on old injustices). None of us are perfect, we all make mistakes. It is from them we learn. Forgiveness is an important part of your relationship. You need to forgive for your own sake, not for the other person's sake. It is not that you accept what someone else has done, but that you yourself need to let go.

It is also important to be able to say I am sorry if you have done something to hurt your partner. A sincerely sorry that really comes from the heart can make wonders. However, the effect of forgiveness looses its power if you use it as a way to try to smooth over repeated mistakes.

When should you forgive and move on, and when should you not? Can one forgive everything is a question I get a lot? There is no right or wrong when you should forgive and when you should not. It has to feel right for you. But to not forgive, creates bitterness in you.

Infidelity is often difficult to forgive and it is usually not that your partner has been with someone else who is the hardest part, it is losing trust, and then you lose your feeling of security. Some choose to forgive infidelity after processing it, others choose to leave.

Whatever you choose, somewhere along the way you will usually come to a crossroad where it is time to forgive. It doesn't have to be the partner you need to forgive it might as well be you who need to forgive your self for ending up in this situation. For most of us it is so much harder to forgive our self than others. We put so much unnecessary blame and shame on our shoulders. Forgiveness is healing, there is a very strong force behind it, it allows you to let go. It allows you to go further. Forgiveness is a process, and it is different for every individual and it can take some time before you are ready.

The Comfort Zone

We all have a comfort zone that we have constructed based on what feels safe and manageable for ourselves. In your comfort zone, you make certain choices and use certain behaviours that give you feelings of security. It feels familiar. You know how it works, what will happen and usually the result. Sometimes you can feel a little half-mad and take a step outside and try something new. Usually after a careful consideration if it is worth the risk to try to stick your foot out. Inside the comfort zone it is cosy and you have a false sense of security and you believe you are in control.

It feels very safe to believe that you are in control, but the fact is you have very little control. Life is constantly changing and your world can change in a few seconds. So what you have in your comfortable home zone is an illusion of a security that is created by yourself. Many of us are afraid to go outside the zone, it does not feel comfortable and you do not know what will happen. To get progress for both yourself and the relationship you need to find new ways to deal with and challenge yourselves. You need to be brave and do things that you never dared to do before. You need to get outside the comfort zone. With courage you grow with courage comes strength. With courage you will change yourself. To dare means creating growth for you.

Maybe you have an ability to believe that you have done something special to deserve disappointments and it is a customary assumption that bad things happen to test you or as payback for something you have done wrong. You may believe consciously or unconsciously not only that other people but also god/universe is judging you. So therefore it is better that you stay within the comfort zone so that nothing negative will happen. But this could not be further from the truth. The truth is that every situation is for your highest good even if it does not feel like it. Universe/the higher power punishes none, there is no one that keeps track of what is happening and there is no one who judges except you.

Do you dare to stick your neck out?
What would you like to do if you had more courage?
What can you do to challenge yourself?

Conflict resolution

An external conflict is a symptom of an inner conflict (it is you who react). The subject can be very simple, but has nothing to do with the actual conflict. It is your memories that are awaken. A tone of voice, gestures or a scent can create feelings in you that make you react. You react with fear, hurt, sad, offended, not listened to and you get uneasy because something is threatened within you.

You need to find out what's the bottom of your problem? Were do it origin from? What is it that makes you react? Is it words, a tone of voice, a temper or characteristics? Which of your needs feel threatened? What can you do to heal your needs?

> What was it that happened?
> Where does the conflict origin?
> When did the conflict come to light for the first time?

What are the symptoms, how does it manifest itself?
What is the impact?
What's the solution?
And even more important do you want to get rid of it?

Good to know is that there is usually a layer of incidents that creates today's symptoms. One problem comes from one incident in your life and underneath there can be another incident and so on. You may have to peal the pedals to get to the bottom.

Both parties have their share of fear in a conflict. It is important that both of you are observing your own part. Try to find where you collide? Describe your versions separately while the other listens. There is no right or wrong, it's about feelings. What will happen if you do not solve the problem? What do you want to achieve, proposed solutions and actions? Does the problem need to be solved together?

If you, as we often do, attack the other party, you create more fear. Fear creates fear. Why did you do that etc? If you instead ask questions like, how did you think, how did this happen, what can you do instead? Then you create a much easier atmosphere and no one needs to go into defence. And if one of you says, you hurt me and starts blaming the other then you don't take responsibility for your own wounds. It is you who allow or does not allow anyone else to hurt you. Love never argues it is always fear who argues in a conflict.

In conflicts, it is extremely important that one of you actively listen when the other speaks otherwise the conflict will flare up again. The main thing is not to immediately resolve the conflict, the key is to get acknowledged in your feeling. You need to get recognition and understanding it is not about right or wrong. It's all about the feeling that hides in the shadow below. If you try to do it this way, you be good mirrors of each other, because if you get help to look at what lies beneath you also get help to heal the wounds. You can really help each other so that you can move forward and the same wound don't have to blow up again in a different situation.

I feel that in every conflict each person has to take responsibility for their own part. As soon as you react, you have a part in what is happening. Somewhere under the surface you have a fear that needs to be confronted and dealt with. If you continue to deal with the symptom, you won't find a solution, you need to look at the underlying root problem to create a new model, a new strategy. Only then can you deal with the conflict in a different and new way. And remember that there is always something to learn from challenges in your life.

> If you feel alone what do you need to feel togetherness?
> If you feel not good enough what do you need to feel worthy?
> If you feel separated from your partner what do you need to feel that you belong?
> If you feel that you have failed how can you feel successful?
> If you feel abandoned what can you do see that you are not alone?
> If you feel fear what do you need to feel love?

If you feel angry, disappointed, sad etc. what feeling is hiding under these symptoms? It is up to you, you can go on managing your life or you can heal your painful memories.

To Cling to Old Injustices

If you repeatedly say words like, you were the one who forgot, you were the one who made the mistake you are most definitely clinging to old injustice. If you in a constructive manner have talked about how you feel, if you feel you have been wronged it should be sufficient and then you need to release it. If it repeats itself perhaps the question should be, how I can help so that it does not repeat itself again instead of blaming.

What has been has been, if the other party has cheated and you have worked it out, it can not be drawn up again and again. Obviously it needs to be processed, but not for ever. Have you chosen to stay in your relationship, there are two choices. You can have faith or choose to not have faith. To say that maybe I could trust you, it depends on what is happening is to have the back door open. And if you have an escape route your partner can feel it and in return is not being able to trust you. The result is that you do not trust him/her either. It becomes a vicious spiral where you both lose. When you expect less, you give less. When you give less, you get less and the circle is closed.

Repeatedly pointing out faults favours no one and it is not love, its fear. Most of your body's cells are replaced at the latest every seven years, so people are constantly changing. To be convicted of old incidents over and over again is to not give your partner a chance. And if you go around thinking that, he/she will not change; chances are pretty small in your eyes he/she will ever change.

> Do you stick to old injustices?
> Why?
> What do you need to do to release them?

Happiness

Today we spend amounts of money on chasing happiness. New clothes, cars, travel, material things, beauty and so on. I believe that satisfaction is the secret ingredients in happiness. I think you can buy happiness in the form of things and experiences that give you satisfaction but with the condition that you also take care of your inside.

When you are satisfied happiness is flowing. You are at ease with yourself and even if difficulties will come your way, you can keep the spirit up and have happiness in other aspects of your life except just this one. You have faith. If you are satisfied, you can much more easily take yourself through grief and change. You know that anger and frustration will fade. If you feel the satisfaction of a new piece of clothing, or find that your new exterior fits with how you feel on the inside. How can this be wrong? Are you doing it for the right reasons? As long as your purpose is not to show of to others, make you feel superior, or hide how you really feel. As long as you do things that make you feel good and happy. But you have to constantly ask yourself the question, what is the purpose of this? Why am I doing this?

I do not need passion to be happy! Anyone who says he/she do not need passion to be happy, I think is lying to himself. I think it is vitally important to have passion in life. Without passion you have no vitality no strength and no happiness. I think there are times in life when we choose not to have passion. And I think that there are times in life when we unconsciously turn off our passion. I had a period when I was known as the ice queen in the corridors at work. I was known for being able to take big, tough decisions without adding an emotional feeling in them. What I did not see then, was that my emotional system was turned off there was no passion in my life. And in relationship I chose a man who was as far from its genuine emotional system that I myself was. I did not have passion in my life, I needed order, control and security. But security became deceptive. If I was not in touch with my feelings and did not feel trust how could I be safe? It didn't add up.

What I did not understand then was that I was not in my feminine energy because I had taken over so many masculine characteristics as possible. I was super feminine in appearance but with a masculine way of doing and thinking. I was always one of the guys. I was definitely not satisfied and constantly had a feeling that something was missing. I had no passion, and simply was not happy.

In a relationship, it is the polarity that provides the spark and without spark eventually dies a part of you in the relationship. When passion is lost in the relationship it decreases in other areas of your life.

The electricity between the feminine and the masculine is necessary to not end up in painful relationships where the results are often an escape or only friendship. It is only when you can be true to your self that you will be able to express your true essence properly. Without polarity no passion! And why should you be content without passion in your life? Why should you not live life to the fully?

For a woman the key to passion is vulnerability. You need to dare to be vulnerable, you need to be 100% safe in all aspects of the relationship. The slightest hesitation regarding security will slowly kill the passion. If you do not feel passion in you're relationship, you are not safe enough or you are not willing to be vulnerable.

I think it is a goal to increase people's level of passion, today we are in so many ways creating unhappy people because we don't know better. But we can all take small steps and choose a life were we can feel passion.

> What makes you happy?
> Make a list! Example; relationships, children, friends, books, nature, movies, walking, exercise, food, music?
> How does a perfect day feel and what are you doing?
> Do you have a favourite place?
> How can you actively choose passion and happiness?
> Are you safe and secure enough to be happy?

Sexual Energy

There is a big difference between having sex with someone and to being in love. To have sex, you only need one other person. It is a purely physical desire; it does not have anything to do with the person you have next to you to do, and not with your inner feelings. And it is where the feminine and masculine behaviour often differ. A woman more often sees (it does not apply to all) sex (and does not distinguish between love) as a way to get a man. A man has easier to see sex as "just" sex, a conquest or a need. And once again you are back to how clear have you been with what you expect, have you listened, and have you understood without putting your own expectations of how it should be?

But I thought it meant something more? What was it that made you think that it meant something more? What was said? In therapy sessions, many of my clients answer, but I took it for granted. You have assumptions on what is right or wrong; you often do not have a clue about what is right or wrong for the other person. Then how can you then feel betrayed? You have not talked about or asked about the rules of the game.

Sometimes you need to realize that the attraction you feel does not mean that you are compatible or spiritually close. The attraction means that you are attracted to one or more similar vibrations of the person you encounter. But the vibration may just affect one area of the other person (emotional, physical, mental or on spirituality level). It does not have to give you everything you need to be a complete relationship.

Sexuality is still today in many ways quite taboo, we like to "play" on sex and are often quite liberated with the wrong purpose (to get attention) or uncomfortable talking about sex. Sexuality is natural, it is a vibrant life force within you, and yet it creates so much fear. It is a very strong energy that has the pleasure to take you to places that you never knew existed.

And as with everything else in life, you have set up rules and guidelines on what is normal and what is not normal when it comes to sexuality. If you believe that you somehow go beyond the norm of what is normal there will be feelings of shame and guilt. Instead you put the lid on and hide, trying to control or even ignore what you feel. It can lead you to block the energy. If you block the energy, the emotions of sexuality can be dead when you have sex because you are so used to turn it off. You block what it is naturally in our body.

A lot of people do not want to get caught in an oppressive sex morals but see themselves as very liberated and some of them are, and rightly so. Others use sex as a way to get confirmation, to get a feeling of being good enough, or as a consolation in the moment, maybe to avoid being alone or to acquire conquests. If you use these reasons to have sex as often as possible, you will exceed your sexual energy. If the reason and the purpose are wrong then the energy will slowly die and when it begins to die, you need more stimulation to feel pleasure. This means that you start chasing it and the more you chase the harder it becomes to find. You do not find satisfaction. You start looking for it in person after person but you will not be satisfied, every new person becomes a disappointment. No one will be able to give you what you want. To come to terms with the sexual energy and keep it alive on a healthy, creative and beautiful level, you need to start loving. You need first of all to love yourself.

Actually, it's about the same areas that you have read in the past chapters to build better relationships. You need to communicate more than perform. You need to let go of fear and dare to look at the things that hurt you, you need to be fully present. You need to let go of all notions of how it should be. It's about learning to ignore everything, let go and follow the flow from within you.

To love is to give without conditions. If you feel it in your body, your heart and your soul you love. If you just feel it in your body then you have a sexual attraction. The difference is significant and can not be hidden from the person you have sex with. And I emphasis this once extra, you can not hide. Your presence or non-presence always feels. To really feel the ecstasy, you must take the risk to let go of all inhibitions, all the fears and trust that the person next to you can meet you in the feeling. It is a spiritual meeting, rather than a physical meeting.

When you no longer feel confident, when you are too afraid, when you put up walls and defences and dare not talk about what you feel, the relationship slowly changes. It happens when you become dependent on your partner, when you are afraid of losing each other or when you are tired. When trust is lost, passion disappears. When you no longer are sharing honesty disappears. Without honesty disappears trust. It's a merry go round. To have a passionate relationship, you need to be truly intimate with each other. Being intimate means sharing your emotions and to be vulnerable.

Each person's sexual energy is different, it follows no rules and norms about what it should or should not be. The energy is beyond all limits. You need to accept yourself as the sexual and sensual creatures that you are. And your attitudes to sexuality is sociological rather than biological, it means you can change it to fit the life you want to live.

Tantra and the Eastern traditions say that the key to making friends with your desire is to centring your attention on the energy itself and not the object of desire. Desire focused on a person can never make you completely happy. This is because what you love touches your passion for something that is beyond the individual - something that is much greater. Human consciousness has roots in the infinite - boundless openness and love. I think this is a very nice way to look at it.

Aware passion means to own your own energy. The point is not to free your self from relationships. Instead, it gives you the opportunity to fully feel the presence and strength in them and become more intimate with others. How close you can come another human being, how intimate you may become depends on how thick walls you have built around you, how many risks you are willing to take and how open your heart is.

> Do you have sex or do you make love?
> Do you confuse lust with love?
> How intimate are you?
> How comfortable and confident are you in your sexuality?
> Do you dare to let go of your inhibitions?

I also would like to write to you some words about oxytocin. Oxytocin is a peptide hormone and acts as a neurotransmitter in the brain and it plays a huge role in social bonding and sexual reproduction in both sexes and especially during and after child birth. It's the love hormone and levels of oxytocin increases during a touch from another person like hugging. An orgasm increase the female's level of oxytocin to a higher level than what a man gets and it is probably why woman tend to have easier to fall in love with a man directly after they have had sex. I think this is good to know because many of my female clients when they have meet someone new immediately think they are in love. It could be the oxytocin speaking.

Feelings

Awareness of your feelings is essential for healing the heart. Emotions are consolidation of thought and emotional energy. They become your beliefs, the stronger the energy the stronger conviction. You have the power in your hands, it is why you need to find out what you really feel.

Today it's common to grow up in families where you do not talk about emotions, you suppress them or you did not get the emotional support that you needed. If you do not learn to talk about your feelings, you learn to shut them up. If no one listens to you or if you get a negative response when you express your feelings, you learn that they are secondary.

Have you lost touch or are you afraid of your feelings? Maybe you are afraid of the strength in them or maybe you are afraid that it will hurt too much if you lift the lid and let them out. So you try to turn them off, suppress them or build walls and defence around you so that no one can access what is within you. The problem is that the emotions will remain within you, they will create blockages in your body and these blockages prevent you from doing things and it can create stress symptoms and diseases in your body.

It is easy to imagine that if you recognize the feelings of revenge or anger, it will turn you into a hateful person. But in fact, the reverse happens as long as you can relate to the negative feelings as something that you have experienced. If you use the same feelings as a weapon to blame and attack others then you become more hatful. If you instead acknowledge your negative emotions, experience and accept them and then let them go. Anguish and emotional suffering is warning signs that you live against your own truth. The point is to get through what hurts.

When you are prepared to fully experience all the feelings that you have, you release the pressure and the blocking force disappears. You need to learn that negative feelings need to be experienced just as much as the positive. When you take a closer look and feel what it is that hurts you get full access to your potential. If you do not dare to feel and block a feeling it builds a resistance in your body, and resistance against an emotion creates an even greater pain than the feeling itself does.

There are no negative or positive emotions, you are the one who put that value on your emotions. All emotions have a function they serve as your natural control system. They tell you truthfully what you are in emotional need of and what you need to change. You need to accept and feel all the feelings that you actually have.

To prove vulnerable is a good way to let the emotions speak whether they are positive or negative. Do not hide behind your fears and hide what you really think and feel. You are worth so much more.

In a relationship you need to have emotional equality. This means that you have the right to own your feelings and to be recognized for them. It does not mean that the other person needs to agree with you. Sometimes you are afraid of what the other person will think if you really say what you feel. You are afraid of being rejected, mocked and maybe inferior etc. But if you start with your feeling, that can never be wrong and are wary of how you express it, then you have taken responsibility and shown what you feel. Then it's up to the receiver to handle it, it is not your responsibility. If only one party in the relationship has a monopoly on expressing and determining when and what is acceptable when it comes to emotional expression you need to do something about it.

Some people are afraid of their negative emotions especially that the feeling of fear will be overwhelming and if those feelings come to the surface that they will never end. The grief, the anger, the pain and the fear will take over and colour their whole life, to get caught up in emotions and never be able to put a stop to them. How long should I be sad? How long will I be angry? Will this never end? But when it comes to relationships, it is usually the suppressed emotions, what you do not want to acknowledge that causes the problem, since they instead take the expression of other fears. And fears create conflicts. If you tune in on your loving mood there would be no conflicts.

I worked with a client who was very frightened. She described it herself as every time her partner was talking with or about any other woman, added a new acquaintance on social media etc in her heart she immediately began to feel ill. A knot in the stomach, she was worried but she did not dare to ask anything because then he would find out how jealous she was. So instead, she kept it within herself, became angry and dismissive until she exploded over something completely different. She created conflicts often over little things instead of telling him that she felt scared. Her fear of abandonment that she experienced at an early age also meant that she provoked the quarrel to see if he would be able to stand firm. She tried in every way to see if it was really her he loved, or if he would leave her. When she found all her fears and the triggers that had happened in her childhood, she decided to talk to her partner and tell him when and why she was so scared. She would also ask for help and say that if I tell you that I am afraid the only thing you need to do is to hold me. To "hold" a nice hug gives many positive effects.

It is showing that you care, that you stand behind and support. It also gives you the glorious hormone oxytocin which is reassuring. At least 20 seconds of a hug does wonders to your body and soul.

Every time you experience one of these unwanted feelings it is a good idea to sit down, relax, close your eyes and try to identify what it is you are feeling right now. Do you feel sad, if yes, ask yourself, why am I sad? Is it the loss of a specific person, concerns about a particular event? Is it about safety or security? Or maybe you feel lonely? Awareness is the source of being able to heal what hurts within you.

Take responsibility for your life and your feelings. If you continue to ignore the negative feelings you are stuck in the illusion that you are powerless. If you do not take full responsibility for the situation you are in, you remain powerless. Take back the power over your life. You need to meet and embrace all that is within you, with love.

If you are honest with your actions, behaviours and weaknesses you can clearly see how you contribute to your partnership with someone else. If you deny what you feel you get stuck and are unable to move forward with your life. Your negative emotions are the answer to why you are not moving forward in your relationships. The key is not to stop feeling emotions but rather to feel every emotion. You need to feel more without getting stuck in an individual feeling for too long. With too long, I mean when you begin to feel bitter, depressed, or that you get anxiety then you need to get help. To feel emotions makes you more alive, it gives you passion and is a major driving force in every aspects of life. And who would not want to live a passionate life instead of a mediocre?

You can handle grief but when grief goes into depression it is the depression that controls you. You can be Angry but when the anger goes into bitterness, it's the bitterness that controls you. Envy can be a positive driving force, but when envy goes into jealousy, it's jealousy that is in control. Learn how to put words on your feelings, feel them and ask for help. Always seek professional help when needed.

Are you good at expressing what you feel?
Are you aware of all your feelings, or are there some feelings that you would rather not acknowledge?
Do you know what the feelings that you do not want to acknowledge origin from?
What can you do to start expressing them?

Promises

We often have promises in a relationship which is implied. Promises that should make you feel secure in your relationship. You should not behave this or that way, we are exclusive to each other, no infidelity. These so-called "rules" are often not expressed but implied, you simply take for granted that things should be in a certain way. If you promise to feel or behave according to certain rules, you sooner or later have to choose between being true to yourself or to the rules. It is almost inevitable that you are not ever going to have to choose. When you stop being honest and true, there is not much left to give in a relationship, in the end you only have an empty shell left, a beautiful promise but no real people.

For many centuries we have taken marriage for granted, that it will last forever, it is part of the promises. Not so long ago (and even in present days) when a couple is going through a divorce the feeling of failure can be quit overwhelming. We did not make it. We did not stay together despite children or common interests, or whatever it may be that you

believed was part of the glue in the relationship that holds everything together. If you instead assume that you meet people to learn, it will be easier to see that separated or divorced couples are not failures. First, I do not think that people in general can be unsuccessful, second, if we go separate ways it can mean two things. Either you have learned everything that you're going to learn from your partner, there is simply nothing more to gain for you to develop. Or you have not dared to dive and look at the wounds that you carry and then you have not had enough confidence in your partner, and if so it is not the right person to experience those things with. There is no failure. It is also about the world spinning rapidly, that development goes much faster and that today you are able to learn your lessons in much less time than you did before.

If you look at it this way they are really a success, you have learned what you should learn and you get faster access to learn what you need elsewhere. It may not be with another person but with yourself.

Do you have a clear vision of what your expectations from your partner and your relationship are? If you don't not know what "promises" you live with and what unspoken expectations you have of him or her, there is a risk that one of you is breaking these promises without even being aware of them. And it feels like something that would be fairly easy to fix?

Separations/Divorces

The way you handle separations and divorces equally depends on how strong your self-esteem is as anything else. I can honestly admit that separations have not been my best side, in some cases, I should if I would have been much more confident and more mature acted quite differently. But I had not the knowledge I have today so I could not handle them in a different way. I have been trying to repair retrospectively.

I am convinced that substantially more "loving relationships" than what we see today can survive a separation. Often it is not that you stop loving someone but that you stop loving the way that you want an intimate relationship to be. If you instead recognize that it is the form of the relationship that changes it's not love that completely disappears. You can continue to love your ex- men and women, but it does not mean that you should have a relationship or that there is an attraction. What if you can feel the uplifting feeling that it's okay to love each other forever?

Helena Källström

Closing the door to the heart, filling it with a lot of unwanted emotions because you are scared and hurt instead of letting it go creates so much unnecessary conflicts. Consider whether it is your heart or you ego that has taken the most damage when you are filled with negative thoughts.

Honesty

How honest are you to yourself? Are you honest in your actions and intentions to yourself and others? How do you know that you are not fooling yourself? Often you do things out of old habit, is an old saying. I say that you are doing things out of an old thought. An old automatic thought that pops up instantly without you even thinking about it, or question yourself. Because we think as we always have, we don't know anything else.

Our automatic thoughts are created way back in time. You create an unconscious decision when something emotionally strong has happened to you and your programming tells you, this is it, this is true, and when something pops up today your thoughts are already pre-programmed, and your reactions come automatically. For example, if you once have been abandoned or cheated by a person with specific character traits and you felt deeply hurt.

What happens when you meet a new person with similar character traits? Probably your automatic thoughts start running at full speed and you feel an uneasy feeling in your stomach? You know something that makes you not trust this person without you even knowing him/ her. Repeat is already tuned in.

What can do you do to challenge and break through old patterns of thoughts? Thoughts that give you preconceptions that are not true and don't benefit you. The easiest way for you to do this is to simply ask yourself, is this really true? Punch holes on the false truth, argue it away, proving it away. Stop as soon as you get a thought that is negative and create anxiety in your body and ask yourself, is this really true, are you absolutely sure? Is it possible there is another answer?

How often do you say yes to things you really want to say no to? You want to be kind, to feel needed. It's a nice feeling to feel appreciated. But what happens if you do the things you do not really want to do? Go to that dinner, family reunion, a course, it's only a few hours, you have to sacrifice yourself at times. How are you feeling? Does it feel good? Or is there some irritation within you that grows? Perhaps you wish that you would have done something else instead? It may also be that if you put up and do this for someone else, your smart brain has an own agenda saying that you owe me a favour later. Are you doing this for someone else, even though you do not want to, so you have one outstanding? How honest is this?

To be honest is to have no ulterior motive when you do things, not to have any purpose other than what you have stated, to be honest with what you want and what you expect. Your agenda is actually what you say and nothing else.

I meet a lot of people and often when we talk about emotions, many of them say that they have good contact with their emotional system. I have empathy, are often said, I cry, I know what I want and like and I stand up for myself tend to be ordinary comments. But if you have empathy for someone else because you can get personal gain from it, if you become sad and cry for someone else to feel sorry for you, or for you to get your own way, then you are not fully honest with yourself. Then you don't have an emotional anchoring, but only a logical. You don't have full contact with your heart. Then you proceed from fear and not from love and chances are that you consciously or unconsciously manipulate to get what you want or to reach your wish.

If you do not want or do not dare to feel the real feelings that you have, one reason may be that you will get consequences that you are not prepared to take. Another of the main reasons that you manipulate is maybe that you unconsciously want control. When a person has stopped using these strategies of manipulation, he or she has very easy to recognize another person using similar strategies. You can recognize the manipulation "game" before someone has barely begun to play.

Honesty can be difficult because you often are not aware that you are dishonest. And it can be a scary world out there if people like and love you when you are not truly honest. How will they think and feel about you when you are? It requires a lot of courage to be honest but to not be not only creates dysfunctional relationships; it can also cost you your own health in the form of suppressed emotions. And suppressed emotions often lead to depression. No one else can tell you what is right or wrong, you are the one paying the bill. It is your own responsibility to take care of your health. What price are you willing to pay for not being honest?

> How honest are you with yourself?
> How honest are you to others?
> What benefits do you get from not being true?
> What does it cost you to not be true?

Living in the Moment

For me, the importance of living in the moment has become a greater and greater need within me. From having lived with sticky notes on what to do tomorrow and searching in the past for solutions to the problem today, to be present here and now. Living in the moment means to me to be just present here and now with my full attention. I can't count the number of times that my daughter has talked to me while I have done other things simultaneously. I could not understand her words, "you're not listening." I thought that I was very good at listening, I heard everything - but I was not fully present. I did my best, but now I know better.

Your mind, your thoughts and what you believe in keeps you often stuck in the past or in the future - with the existence in the heart. If you live in tomorrow, you either worry about something that will happen or you look forward to something that will make you happy in any form. If you live in yesterday, you have wounds that hurt or you remember moments of happiness or regrets. It does not matter which, because you have lost the present moment. You are not here and now. To constantly look for answers, dreaming forward or worry solves nothing of what is happening here and now. Because you do not give the feeling that is here and now, the acknowledgment that it needs. You miss life!

Of course, you should look forward to events and of course you sometimes need to go back in time and look at what has happened in your history, but if you miss today you miss to enjoy all of that is actually going on around you.

I am a mindfulness instructor and I believe in the benefits of mindfulness and meditation. Mindfulness is a state of non-judgmental, breathing and relaxation techniques to become more present and aware. These are proven techniques and with a lot of underlying research behind. It teaches you not only to become more aware it also provides great results in various states of diseases; stress, high blood pressure, immune system and depression to name a few. It also creates changes in brain activity, which means you can inhibit the signals that are active in the management of a number of negative emotions. For me meditation can be used in two different ways. It can make me aware and make me feel or I can use it as letting go of awareness. I can be one with everything and flow.

It is so amazing to actively choose to be conscious. To really feel how your food taste, a ripe mango, the smell of an apple, the smell of spices, what sound do you hear when you are really listening, what colours do you see, what do you feel on your skin? I love the wind that blows through my hair when I take the time to feel on my hiking tours, the grass that tickles beneath my bare feet on a warm summer day. As much as I like to swim in velvety sea and see the moon glitter. It is heaven for my senses and relaxing for my heart and soul. We all need this kind of experiences from our hectic day to day life.

Are you present in the moment, or stressing about something that has happened or will happen?

Where are your thoughts right now?

Are you daydreaming about things and events that will happen in the future?

Are you worrying about things that already have happened?

Practice in becoming aware of the moment - capture moments, stay here and now, feel and live as present as you can. It really helps you get a healthier lifestyle.

Should I Stay or Should I Go?

Sometimes you feel that something is wrong in your relationship. Most relationships have obviously ups and downs, good and worse moments, but ask your self what emotions dominate? Do you feel vital and stimulated, or exhausted and worried? How does it feel between the both of you, do you have similar beliefs, values, or does your partner have qualities that complement yours? When you imagine that you are going to spend the rest of your life together (if you use this term to describe a lasting relationship) with this person how does it feel? Love, respect, honesty, confidence and compassion should be the cornerstone of a good relationship. A happy relationship is created when two people are emotionally open with one another and striving that the relationship should be stimulating for both. For this to happen, both need to take responsibility, be mature and positive in the relationship.

The feeling of drifting apart is quite common in intimate relationships, and it may be because you do not listen to yourself and communicate your own needs. Or that, what you want in a relationship and what you actually need are two different things and that you have made a mistake and mixed them together. Perhaps your differences caught up with you and create alienation and loneliness?

Sometimes when you think the question, should I stay or should I go? It's a battle between the heart and the intellect. On one hand, you know, but on the other hand, you feel, which should you listen to, which is the strongest and what is true? Love should be the foundation in intimate relations. Do you love your partner? And has your partner the ability to love you back? You should not only have a partner with a personality that suits you, you also need a partner with good character. A person's character can often been seen on how that person treats himself, and how interested he or she is of being in a loving relationship.

You also need to know or become aware that you do not stay or run away from the relationship because your own wounds are unhealed or that you do not dare to take a closer look at them. Most of us tend to be good at limiting ourselves to what we are willing to see, feel and know about ourselves.

When thinking about whether you should stay or go, it is common that it is a long process before you can make a decision, especially if there are children in the relationship. Very often I get the question, how long should I stay for the sake of the children? My answer is that we should not stay in a relationship for the sake of someone else, not even our children. Most kids feel every little emotional shift that we have and they feel much worse to have unhappy parents living together than separated parents who are happy.

> In your relationship consider what you yourself have to offer? Some good questions to ask your self might be,

Do I give what I want from a partner?
Do I expect more than what I give?
Do you feel genuine happy in your relationship?
Is he or she emotionally there for you?
Can you be honest?
Do you get support?
Are you getting your needs met?
Do you trust him or her?
Do you feel safe?

Am I Ready to Meet Love in the Shape of a Partner?

When you search for a partner, the first question you have to ask yourself is, what do I constantly get that I no longer want? Characteristics that you've already meet in a partner

The answer gives you an identification of what you need to work on. What was the common denominator in your past relationships that attracted you? What were the advantages and disadvantages in the relationship?

I can honestly say that I have faced my worst fears and I have met my brick walls. I have met traits from my mother, my father and my grandfather. And you need not be a genius to realize that I was not very mature in those meetings. But as much as I have confronted my worst fears, I meet my best sides. The problem for me was that it took a long time to realize that I could use these meetings to heal and not to put up even a higher wall around myself.

You meet the people you need to meet at the emotional level you are right now. (I know I'm repeating myself a lot.) The less you have come to terms with yourself the more messed up relationships you will have. This is why it is so important to work on your self. It does not matter if you're looking for the first relationship or the tenth.

Some of you do not like to look at what has been, but if your old relationships still affect you, they have a meaning in your life now. Are you still mad at your ex and pondering on this, or do you still feel misunderstood in your old relationship? Then it's time to clear away all the old rubbish that remains and grow so that you do not take it with you into the next relationship. Are there traits from your parents that repeat themselves? Is it your fear that makes you attracted to a certain personality type? Is it your own favourable sides you see in a potential partner? Is there a certain appearance that you find attractive?

Have you come to terms with your fears so that you can go into a new relationship and be open and curious? If you honestly dare to admit and look at what went wrong in previous relationships and why you react and act like you do in the present, you get the first insight to change. It is only then that you take responsibility for your part in what went less well in past relationships. And it is only then that the next relationship can be better,

If you want to get as much as possible out of a relationship; you need to give it space.

You need to give it space in everyday life and you need to give it space in your thoughts and, above all, in your emotions. A close relationship is not something you can turn on and off when it suits you. It's with you all the time. Do you want an exclusive relationship, you need to let go off "all the others" if there are such and dare to invest. You can not have the cake and eat it if you want to have lasting relationships. If you are not prepared to do this you need to be honest about it.

You unconscious strategies are often tricky. You can be pretty confident that you are ready for a new relationship but are still not finding the right one. You might be searching and searching but only finding fault in everyone.

One of my clients talked constantly about how much he longed for a partner. The loss he described as enormous and he spent a lot of time to focus on prospective partners, but as soon as he met someone it just flowed out in the sand. He is a very good looking man, and described himself as he never ever had trouble finding women. The reason he came to see me was that he did not feel any emotions when he met a woman. He described the candidates as very nice and very good-looking women, but there was no energy, no passion. When we looked at what was happening, it turned out that this talkative, very social man built up a variety of protection around him so that no one could get close. He was the one that all who encounter him for the first time thought was very confident. Outwardly, he was the perfect mother in law dream that everyone fell for, and he was looking feverishly to find someone that he would fall in love with. When we put together piece after piece in the puzzle of what kind of feelings and thoughts that appeared when he met someone, slowly a new picture took shape. A picture of a man who did everything he could to not find a woman to commit to. A man who came from a relatively safe upbringing and where he during a hypnosis session found that the person closest to him, in this case his mother that he mentally trusted, actually had not been reliable at all. These were memories that he had completely repressed. He searched with his logical thinking security and stability in woman but his subconscious emotional system, said you can not trust women. There are many times that appearances are deceptive, that our subconscious has a different agenda than your conscious have. In a case like this it does not help to have the best intentions in mind if you do not heal the unconscious memory and the feeling behind it.

The deeper more authentic self-knowledge you have, the more you get to know yourself, the stronger the emotional intelligence you also look for in a mate. This means that the range of potential partners narrows when you see yourself in a new light. You are no longer content with superficial contacts you need to meet someone who you feel is on your new emotional level.

Ask for Help

How many times have you wished, created goals and visions or set your intention on dreams that have not come true? You had a vision; all the candles were lit._You have made a note in the calendar for when things should be ready, repeated affirmations in the mirror. And it has really felt like a pretty good start, right? And then other things pop up and come you way and you do not get the results you were aiming for. You should have had your website completed a specific date, but the date has already passed and the website is still not finished. You should have a workshop filled with people - and no one signed up. You finally launched your e-book but got zero sales. So what happened?

Usually, there are things you could have asked for, but you did not. Because when it comes down to it, you are afraid to ask for help. Maybe you're afraid to ask for help because you think others have a picture of you as a strong person who can do it all by yourself? Maybe you show an image of yourself that is not true in reality?

Do you reject all offers of help? Do you find it hard to accept? What if someone offers to buy you a cup of tea or lunch how do you feel? There is a little-known but still vital secret that allows you to get growth and abundance. Ask for help!

Many of us have been brought up in a patriarchal society that taught you that strong and independent means to work hard and to never ask for help. Some also learn that to ask for and receive help is the ultimate sign of weakness. Asking for help is a failure, and if you do ask, you feel inadequate. Instead, you are programmed to do, do, do and give, give, give as if you do not deserve to ever get your needs met. And so you give until you begin to neglect your own needs. Your ability to receive is directly related to your happiness which is reflected in your bank account and success.

Need help? No, thank you, I manage, I'm fine!

Maybe you do not want to ask for help because, you do not want to be interpreted as selfish, you do not want to be a burden to others, you believe that full independence is admirable. You also may believe that if you would make success and succeed despite difficulties, it is even more admirable.

So how do you turn the page so that you are not afraid to ask for help and get the support that you sometimes need? It is quite simple if you only dare. You need to stop waiting for someone to offer you help. Stop complaining about what you do not get, and ask for what you need. Stop getting other people to guess what you need and be specific. Be humble and grateful!

Ask for help whenever you need! Can you help me with...? Would it be possible...? I need help with...?

Balance in life

During a period when I worked as a manager and was facing a tough re-organization, I got a mentor. She was a priest and she would coach me through a tough time with many decisions and emotions. She began this first meeting to talk about the importance of having balance in life. She illustrated balance in life in the form of a cake which was cut open with all its pieces. Then we filled these pieces of content such as work, relationships, family, hobbies, etc. and talked about the importance of getting all the pieces in a satisfied size to feel good. In this period, I had no balance in my cake. I had a piece that was dominant and the remaining pieces were quite small and some virtually non-existent. When I talked to her, I realized that I actually was not feeling well. I had no breathing space. I knew I was stressed but I blamed it on external factors and did not realize that it was my own choice.

Since the meeting with this amazing woman, I try to have balance in my life. Of course, it happens that one piece stands out and becomes very large or very small in periods but I try to get them to the size I want. But I have also thought a lot about if it is only balance in life that we need? I think we need both balance and integration. We need to integrate the pieces into each other for life to work optimal for us.

Balance in life is a choice that you yourself need to take responsibility for. You need to make sure that you take time to fill your pieces of the cake with meaningful content. Work, family, friends, hobbies, and fun, things you like to do, to make sure you have a good mental and physical health. Some have spirituality in their pieces of cake, it can be about religion, meditation or yoga.

When you are able to do things you like to do, whether it is about reading a book in the hammock, sitting in a cafe, planting geraniums or carpentry, you load your depots of satisfaction, happiness and love. And you can in the next step share with others all the beauty and inspire change.

When you feel love, you want to share it with the world. Charity is also something that gives a lot of satisfaction. Contributing does not mean that you need to contribute money, you can contribute your knowledge or your time. There are many organizations with volunteer work.

Do you live a balanced life? An inspiring way is to take pen and paper and draw how your cake looks, are there any pieces missing? What size do you want them to have? Decide how you want your life to be, what content do you desire? What choices do you need to take to make you feel satisfied? How can you achieve your goals? Be honest, listen to yourself and write down what you really want. There is a big difference in what we hope to achieve in life and what we decide to reach. How would a person who only knows love for himself choose his life?

Sometimes you lose your balance when there is too much stress. Too much work, too much pressure, too complicated relations, illness and other things that take a toll of your life.

Try to find peace by taking a moment and breath. Concentrate and feel the present. (Deep, slow breaths through your nose, close your eyes please). Slow down, breath through any pain let the stress leave your shoulders. Sit for as long as you need. Just concentrate on your breathing. With every breath you can feel the tension slowly living your body. Shift your focus and ask yourself, how do I feel? Are you feeling stressed, tired, sad, angry, etc. Just note and try not to put a valuation on what you feel.

> Which is the best choice for me right now?
> Which direction is the best way for me to go?
> What do I need to do to make a change?

Does your outer life, the side you show to the external world difference with who you really are? Then you have lost control and live a life that is determined outside of you. To not live in accordance with your self creates bitterness, voids and a generally bad mood. Feelings of wishing you were somewhere else. You are looking for something, anything that can fill the void in your heart. Just as there are no relationships outside of you, there is no problem outside yourself. Don't go around and feel hollow, there is help to get.

It's up to you to change, to achieve what you want, you need to take responsibility for yourself. You may have heard the expression "It's never too late to get a good childhood."

There is some truth in this expression. Your past is always with you but it is up to you how it manifests itself, and above all, how you handle it. Many are those who have managed to turn tragic childhood experiences into success stories.

Turn Your Dreams Into Reality

If someone asks you, you can probably list many things that you would like to have on your" bucket list", "100 Things to do before I die" list. Think of all the things that you are passionate about and imagine your life full of them. Decide what you want to do and turn your dreams into reality. Dreams can be as grand as any, and who's to say that they are unattainable? If you follow someone else's dreams or ideas on how it should be, you create yourself an existence but you do not create a life. Above all, what you create is not your own life. Make sure it's your own life that you live even if it is not in alignment with those close to you.

Imagine the happiness of fulfilling all these dreams. If you can see yourself in your dream and you know it's something you really want in your life - go for it. Do not let anyone or anything stop you. And don't wait for the right time, the right time is now.

Identify your dreams large and small. What do you want? What is really important to you? How does it feel? See it. Taste it. Ask for it. Talk to yourself, your diary, your closest friends, the universe, the trees and your dog. It can be about personal development, relationships, travel, living, work. Imagination has no limits. Then begin to sketch a rough draft of how to get there. Use a large sheet of paper, sketch, draw, paint, paste up cut-outs and pictures of your dreams. Allow yourself to believe that nothing is out of reach. Dream big, set no limits, not even the sky is the limit. Dream beautiful and dream fun. If you want to succeed you need to stop thinking realistically and broaden your mindset that anything is possible.

Make a step-by-step plan for how you will achieve your dream. Start with the major details and work your way down to every nook and corner. Make sure you have a foolproof plan in place before you start your journey. But although you have a foolproof plan it will require improvisation and spontaneity. Once you have your plan in place its time for you to take action. Realize your dreams by imagining how happy you will be when you reach yours goals, how proud you will feel.

What can you do in the near future (set a deadline) to get one step closer to your dream? Need to contact someone, write to someone, find a new hobby, save money, educate yourself, etc. A good goal is characterized by something that affects and touches your emotions. It is absolutely crucial to success. Do you know someone who knows someone? Brainstorm ideas, what kind of network do you have around you, stretch out a hand and see if someone can help you. What can you do today (don't postpone) that will allow you one step closer to your goal? Anything that helps you get one step further on the way?

Next step is to make a written our talk out loud order to the Universe. I'm ready and plan to implement this. I plan to "travel to the moon". I am grateful for all the help I will get.

Then let go! Have faith that what you sow, you will reap. Keep an open and loving mind.

Sometimes your dreams pop up in another better shape than you originally ordered. If you feel setbacks at times and it doesn't go as fast as you want, setbacks are a part of the process. It is how you react and act to setbacks that bring you one step closer to the goal. Take control of your thoughts and guide them to a positive challenge. If you choose to think that you will find a solution, you will find a solution. And remember that if you want something you've never had before, you need to change and do something you have never done before.

Back to the Power of your Thoughts

Why is it that sometimes you shrug your shoulders on something that another day would make you very sad? The difference is the state you are in. The truth is that it is you who are the source of your own state of mind, you have the ability to control, influence and change your condition. You are not your state of mind you can choose which state you want to be in.

What would happen if you only think good thoughts about yourself and other people? How different would the world appear? How different would you see yourself? Are you willing to mentally create a different image of yourself? Changing your thoughts one by one? How happy would you be? How much love and joy would you feel?

And if you can change the world with your thoughts, how harmful is your negative beliefs? In 1993 an eight-week test was made with meditation to bring down crime in Washington. The result was that crime dropped by 23.3%, an incredible figure.

For those of you who have not seen the photographs of Dr. Masaru Emoto (Waters hidden messages), I recommend this book. Amazing photographs of ice crystals in water, formed differently if they get exposed to positive or negative messages. I am convinced that you can affect so much more than you think and do today. The same goes for your relationships with other people. Relationships are mental and emotional structures. A feeling is awareness of a vibration. They are created, it's your choice.

When it comes to something that you want to change in the long term, the key to creating new habits is having a clear picture of what you want to create, you need to believe that what you want is better than what you have (maybe you have to create a new belief around you abilities), a feeling of being truly worthy and make a plan before start, it will make changes so much easier

What would you have to think or do differently in order to feel more security, happiness and love? The reason that you maintain a behaviour that you want to get rid of or change is that it satisfies a need on some level. It is easier to be a victim of circumstances then to take responsibility over your life.

It's all about awareness of your thoughts and behaviours, and then finding better options which give you the same kind of effect, or better yet, exceed them. Finding your emotional blockages and heal them so that it does not affect you in relationship with others. Making conscious choices which you choose based on love. You have an incredible ability to change what you think and if you change what you think you will feel differently. And in the next step, you will act differently. It's amazing what you can influence to have a happier and more satisfying life. Love can not be found outside of you it's already in you if you have the courage to face this incredibly wonderful, powerful energy.

Walt Disney said, those who do not believe in magic will never find it. The word magic means to "light up" to believe in miracles and how you will get your life to shine. How much magic do you choose to have in your life?

Conclusion

When we meet, soul to soul as pure essence of pure openness and love, we are one. My openness is no different from your transparency, because transparency does not have a solid form and therefore there is no boundary that separates us from each other. Being one, gives moments of bliss in a union of absolute love. No other soul can give you love and touch you unless your heart is open. To get a better relationship with your self is to begin to think of yourself as love itself. Think of your self as both a transmitter and a receiver of an infinite amount of life-giving energy, and then share that love with others. When you feel love and are safe your heart send out loving electromagnetic fields from you and it interacts with the energy fields that we all share. When you have fun it creates positive changes in your energy and you form your physical reality - and as benefits it creates nitric oxide and endorphins in your body that makes you happier.

When you are love, you are not drained of energy and you do not need other people's approval to feel loved. To truly love your self is to know and accept who you are.

A relationship is supposed to be a partnership between two individuals that strengthen each other and help each other to be the best version of them selves. A relationship should not be the result of two half people trying to complement each other.

Choose to love every day and in every breath, true love has no limits. You have an endless source within you, a source that can provide you with all the love that you want and you no longer need to walk around and hope to find the love of your life. Love is a force that can enhance and beautify. It is a force that can get you to accomplish the most incredible things. Just imagine how the world would look like if you continually choose a loving choice. What miracles would happen? And the greatest miracle of all is you. It is you who possess the power to create more love.

It hurts my heart to look back at the many times in my life when I felt that I was not "good enough". I was so hard on myself, unnecessarily. I know I'm not alone in judging myself and trying to fit in when I really should have stood out as the stunning human being that I am. I meet many clients who have the same difficulties to feel adequate and where fear control their choices in life. If I could I would wave a magic wand and global undo all the harsh judgments that we give ourselves. But then I realize I don't have to, because we all possess that magic wand.

The insight is not to find yourself without more to choose yourself and to shape yourself the way you want to be. The truth is that we need to find our own source of love and create a new path free from fear. Abandon hope and always choose a little more love. I promise you my love that the love you seek, is searching for you too.

Epilogue

A new book is finished, a new chapter in life is complete. I turn the page and find new opportunities and challenges. I am so amazed at how strong the power of love is and what opportunities we ourselves possess to influence everything that happens around us. We are in truth the creator of our lives. I do my best to live accordingly to this gift and actually practice what I teach, it is not always easy and I don't always get it right but I have the best intentions.

I wish you love!

Acknowledgement

Mia Fransson, FraMia Design for friendship and turning ideas into reality. I love our creativity meetings and I can not thank you enough for all your help with stunning design and photos. Mia is the one who created this gorgeous book cover with a photo she took of my hands. You can see Mia`s beautiful creations on Instagram and Facebook as framiadesign.

Malin Rosén and Emelie Lagerborg for friendship and never ending conversations about the meaning of life and relationships.

Erika Pettersson sending you love and I'm always by your side.

Nicole my amazing daughter and a permanent teacher. I love you!

Thank you for letting me love you, and thank you for loving me.

And thank you to all my clients who teach me so much and give me the privileges to get to know their life stories. For this I am so grateful.

Bibliography

McTaggart Lynne, The Field; The Quest for the Secret Force of the Universe

Bowlby John, A secure base

Emoto Masaru, The Miracle of Water

Reviews of How to Find Love

I highly recommend this book; it illuminates all the parts we need to look at to create more love in our lives (relationships, sexuality, male, female). I would like all young adults to get this book in their hand.

Helena Källström, you are a great relationship therapist and the book is equally amazing. Thank you for everything you have taught me and the support you gave me.

I recommend this book to anyone who wants to improve their relationships.

I have received a lot of tips that I can use in my relationship. Thank you for responding to my questions.

This is a book that everyone should read. The book is about you!

It's the only book you need.

Helena writes with recognition throughout the book, thumbs up.

About the author

Helena Källström is a Swedish hypnosis and relationship therapist in cognitive behavioural therapy. She has published 2 books in Swedish and How to find love is her first book in English.

Helena has a background of leadership and management working as a manager in different companies in Stockholm. She also has long experiences working with private clients in therapy in her own company AWAreness Leadership. She has been the CEO for a company educating coaches, relationships-, hypnosis therapists and therapists for the 12 steps addiction treatment program. Helena's passion is to help clients find a healthy balance between body, mind, spirit and emotions through awareness.

Helena has been a guest on Swedish radio shows as an expert on relationships, co-dependency and woman leadership. She has had courses, lectures and retreats in Sweden and in Spain.

With her easy reading you get more knowledge and the tools to make healthy changes and find what you are searching for.

Books by the author Helena Källström

I skuggan av livet – a book about co-dependency
Med hopp om kärlek – how to find love

Contact and more information;

www.helenakallstrom.com
www.awarenessleadership.se
Instagram and Facebook; helena kallstrom

Printed in the United States
By Bookmasters